The Sydney We Love

Captain Arthur Phillip RN
First Governor of New South Wales, 1788-92

The

RUTH PARK AND

Sydney We Love
CEDRIC EMANUEL

NELSON

Thomas Nelson Australia
480 La Trobe Street Melbourne Victoria 3000

First published 1983
Text copyright © Ruth Park 1983
Illustrations copyright © Cedric Emanuel 1983

National Library of Australia
Cataloguing-in-Publication data:

Park, Ruth.
    The Sydney we love.

    Includes index.
    ISBN 0 17 006253 8.

    1. Sydney (N.S.W.) – Description – 1976– –
    Guide-books. I. Emanuel, Cedric 1906– .
    II. Title.

919.44'10463

Printed in Hong Kong
by Thomas Nelson & Sons Ltd.

Obelisk 1857 Elizabeth Street

Contents

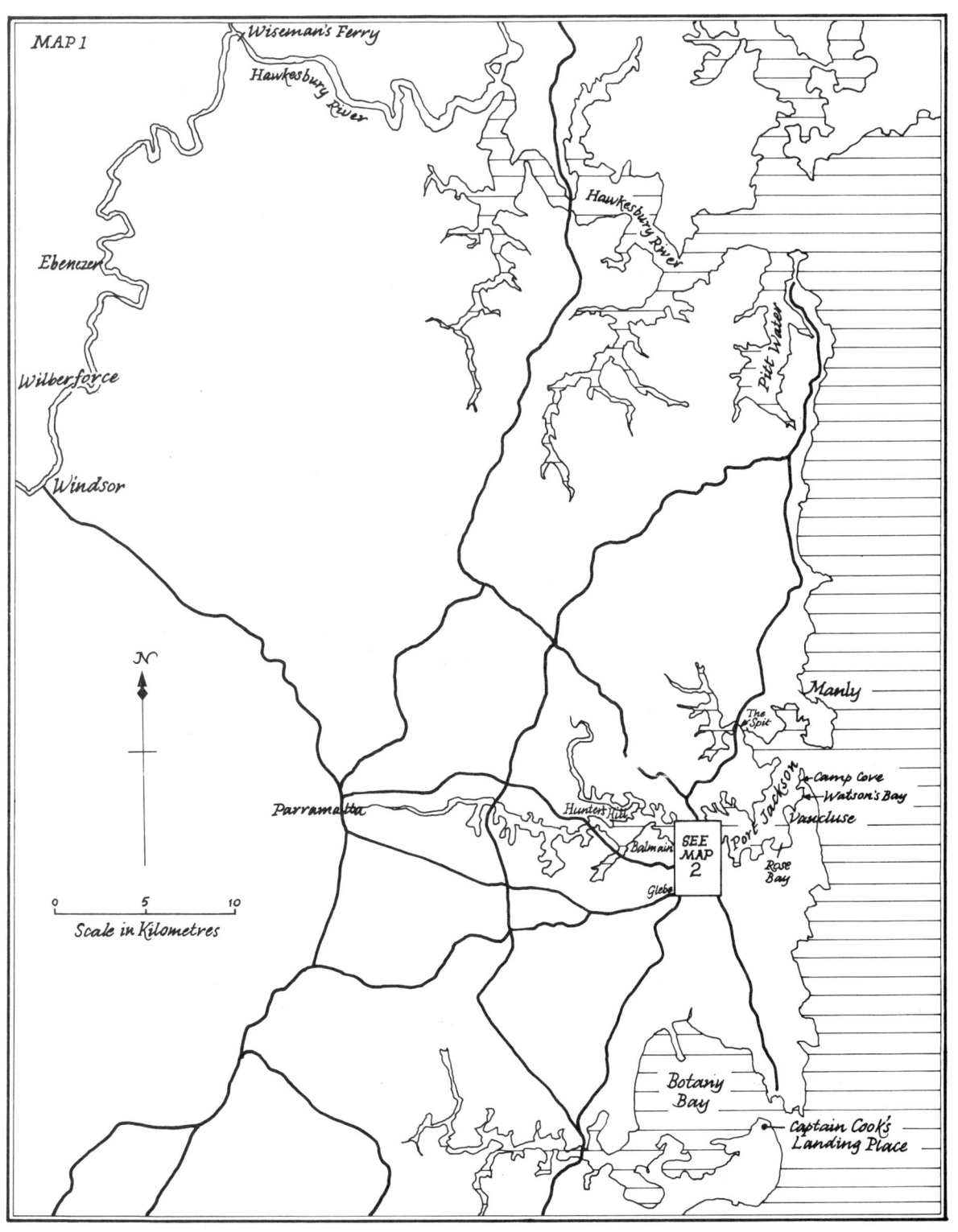

MAP 1

Wiseman's Ferry

Hawkesbury River

Hawkesbury River

Ebenezer

Pitt Water

Wilberforce

Windsor

Manly

The Spit

N

Camp Cove
Watson's Bay

Parramatta

Hunters Hill

Vaucluse

Balmain

SEE
MAP
2

Port Jackson

Glebe

Rose
Bay

0   5   10
Scale in Kilometres

Botany
Bay

Captain Cook's
Landing Place

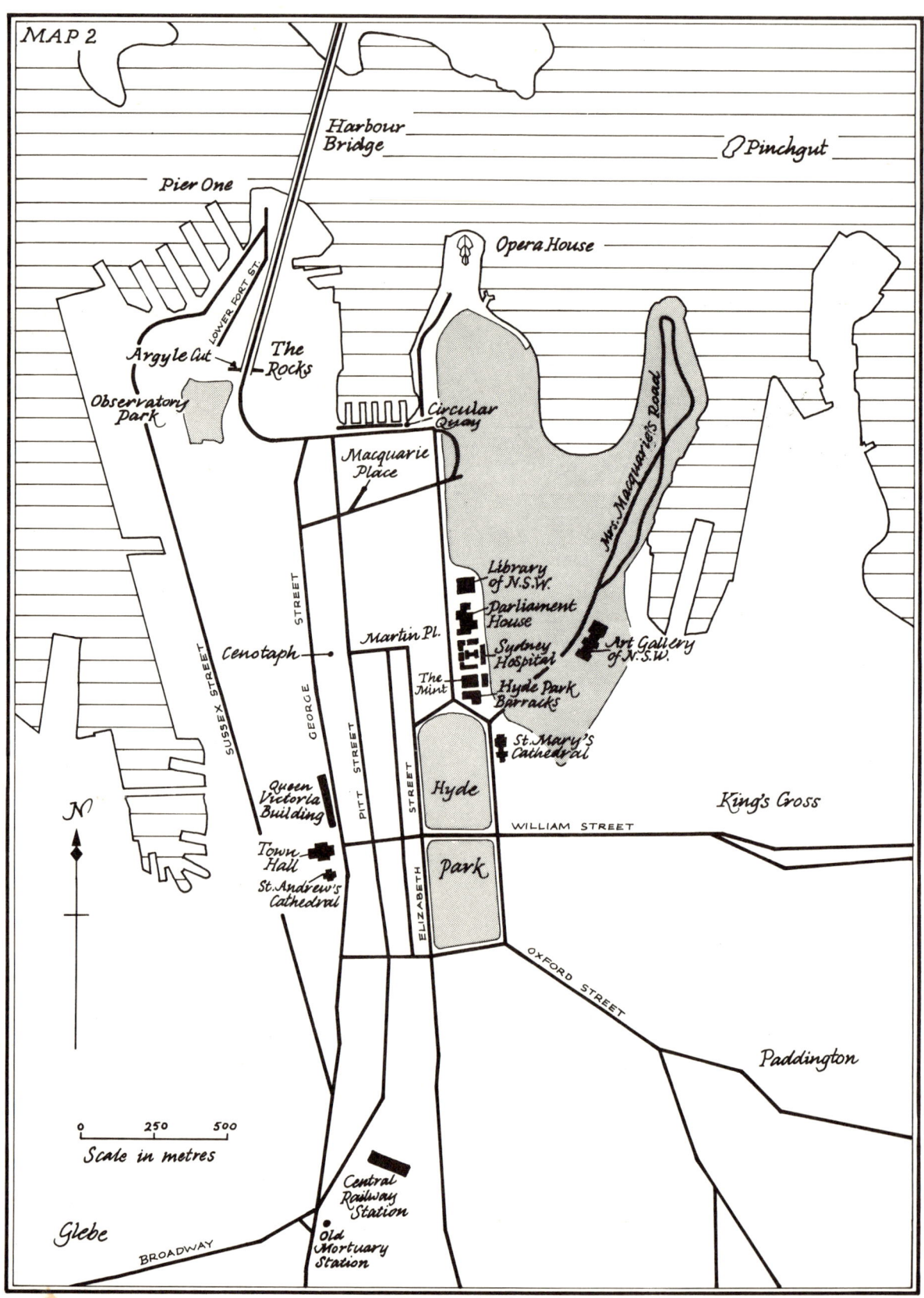

Introduction

Sydney is built on a landscape littered with human bones. Indeed it might never have been born at all if England hadn't been in a pickle after the American War of Independence, finding herself without a penal destination for her stirrers and scallywags, forgers and pickpockets. Thus was the village founded, the first convict settlement in the South Seas, daughter of the American Revolution, the last, loneliest and saddest place on earth. Or so it was planned to be.

But Sydney turned out quite otherwise. Blithe, irresponsible, slightly mad, she has air full of electric sparks, her birds shout in boys' voices, the sunshine is here more often and lasts longer. And even when the bushfire lights her domestic facades as though for some hellish *son et lumière*, you feel it's right, characteristic somehow, Sydney.

Sydney was born near present-day Circular Quay, in a January thunderstorm, 1788, when Captain Arthur Phillip raised the flag for England and christened these waters Sydney Cove. Phillip, son of a German schoolmaster, rose out of a worthy but unpublicised naval career to become the hardworking, infinitely finicky Father of a Nation.

'Upon my soul,' said one of his contemporaries 'I do think God Almighty made Phillip on purpose for that place, for never did man know better what to do, or with more determination see it done.'

He was a little man with a big nose and large 18th-century eyes, and suffered sorely from seasickness.

Captain Phillip had been directed to found his convict colony on the shores of Botany Bay. Very soon he discerned that this place was entirely unsuitable. He explored the great harbour to the north, Port Jackson, made up his mind as to the place of settlement, and returned at once to Botany Bay, where the fleet lay. He was horrified to discover two French warships outside the bay. They were La Pérouse's *Astrolabe*

and *Boussole*, on a scientific expedition. Aware of France's intense interest in Pacific land-grabbing, Phillip must have endured anxious hours. He returned at once to Port Jackson, leaving most of the fleet to follow him. Early in the morning of 26 January he had a flagstaff erected, and 'the English flag, with all that it connoted' fluttered upon the nor'-easter.

A charming account of this great day in Sydney's history is given by James Scott, a Sergeant of Marines. He wrote: 'Saturday, January 26, 1788. At a.m. the fleet got on their way. Came to an anker at ½ pt 6 O'clock in Port Jackson close to the New town which was crisned this day and 4 vollies of small arms fired.' A few mugs of porter were drunk to the colony's success and 'ye whole gave three cheers'.

Is it possible for us to imagine Sydney Cove as it was that day? 'Every man stepped from the boat literally into a wood,' said David Collins, Captain of Marines.

The 'run of clear water' which had made Phillip choose Sydney Cove for a settlement flowed down from the extensive swamps which lay where Hyde Park is now. We do not know what the Aboriginals called this beautiful year-round stream which ran in a deep ferny gully to the Cove, widening into a broad tidal estuary somewhere in the vicinity of modern Pitt Street and its western buildings. Phillip, who caused tanks to be cut in its sandstone bed in order to conserve water, called it the Tank Stream, a hideously utilitarian name. All round the rivulet stood a majestic forest of Sydney red gums, huge myrtles with flesh of luminous rosiness. There were mimosas (speedily renamed 'wattle' because these small flowering trees were the first to be cut down and used in wattle-and-daub huts), and there were also turpentines, ironbark, blackbutt, and the strange grass tree or blackboy, lifting its lance rimmed with downy light.

Soon the settlers were to destroy the Tank Stream itself. Having no knowledge of semi-tropical water storage systems in spongy topsoil and decayed vegetation, they stripped the land bare, hoed up the shallow earth, and in no time lost that as well by erosion. But on that first 26 January all was calm, fertile and, being January, alive with bird and insect life.

Only the sandstone bones of the land remain. The hills have become slighter in grade, the gullies filled, the sea driven back, a forest of steel and concrete cacti has sprung from the rind of the earth.

Circular Quay

Courthouse, Circular Quay

Only a few decades ago Circular Quay was old-fashioned, austere and spacious, rimmed by Victorian buildings with occasional pockets of simple early colonial warehouses and woolstores. This was, in effect, the Quay (though he called it Semi-Circular Quay), created by the brisk military engineer, Colonel George Barney, who between 1837-44 tackled the colossal task of providing the colony with utilitarian waterfront facilities.

Barney had long engineering experience in the West Indies. With vigour and imagination he directed the filling in of the Tank Stream estuary, reclamation of the mudflats, the dredging and deepening of Sydney Cove. He had an unlimited supply of forced labour, and indeed Circular Quay is the last and greatest convict structure to be completed in the colony.

The building of the Quay marked the beginning of the marvellous clipper era. For thirty years the world's fastest sailing ships tied up at the Quay, and fortunately we have many exquisite paintings and hand-tinted lithographs of this era. Circular Quay, then and for another eighty or ninety years, was a majestic front door to a truly maritime city. But in the late 1950s and 1960s reconstruction began again. The Cahill Expressway and City Overhead Railway stride overhead, closing off the sea from the city and the city from the sea that begot it. Magnificent woolstores and warehouses came down, and in the ruins of their foundations demolishers found all kinds of cherishable junk, George III copper coins, soldiers' buttons and bayonets; bits of worm-eaten ship's gear; a convict's tin mug, leaf-thin with rust.

The Quay remembers many polling-booth riots, and one in particular in which the standing candidate, a wealthy ship-owner, restored order by bringing up reinforcements from his whalers, armed with harpoons. In another exceptionally violent riot in the 1880s, thousands of demonstrators thronged the Quay in an attempt to prevent six hundred

Chinese immigrants from landing. They had already been rejected in Port Melbourne. A large number of the frail black-clad figures on the ships were tailors destined for the sweat-shops so numerous in Victorian Sydney. The protestors won the day.

The immense spaciousness of the Quay has been inter-rupted by bus shelters and other modern structures, but still, standing with back to the ferry wharves, the observer can appreciate the felicitous openness that once prevailed between wharves and the Customs House. Built in 1885, designed by James Barnet of the General Post Office and the ornate Lands Department Building, the Customs House is harmoniously proportioned. The double-pillared colonnade, the wrought-iron panels, are simple and dignified, and the portrait head of Queen Victoria and the carved coat of arms very fine. The Customs House would make a suitably placed maritime museum.

To the west of Circular Quay is the old quarter of The Rocks, with all its quaint and historic sights. To the east is the gigantic gleaming butterfly, the Sydney Opera House.

Herald Square
CIRCULAR QUAY
SYDNEY

Cedric Emanuel

The Harbour Bridge and the Opera House

Until the Opera House was built on the eastern horn of Circular Quay, Sydney's sign and symbol was the Old Coat-hanger, the Harbour Bridge. Though it is now an elderly structure, it is still the world's largest single-span bridge. It took less than nine years to build and cost just over $19,000,000. The majestic pylons, so Egyptian in design and colour, reflect their period. Tutankhamen's tomb had just been discovered, and a wave of enthusiasm for Egyptian artforms influenced architecture, fashion and crafts.

Hermit Bay

HARBOUR.

Cedric Emanuel

The Bridge is the visible sign of Sydney's resolutely bilateral development. From the beginning, the harbour which brought such swift industrial and commercial growth to the infant settlement meant laborious travel to those who lived along its shores.

A harbour bridge was a dream constant throughout Sydney's early days. There was also a vociferous tunnel party.

All varieties of bridge were suggested through the years, truss, suspension and even floating. In 1900 the Minister for Works invited competitive designs and tenders for a bridge. Twenty-four were submitted, but the project was shelved. Not until 1922, after considerable parliamentary shuffling, was official approval given to the plan submitted by J.J.C. Bradfield, chief engineer of the Metropolitan Railway construction department.

It is characteristic of Sydney's happy-go-lucky methods of doing things that this extraordinary engineering project was embarked upon when the approaching Depression must surely have cast a prophetic gloom over the future. It is to the credit of the government of the time that work on the Bridge went on, from 1923, when the unemployed percentage of the workforce fell slightly short of ten per cent, to 1932, when the Australian unemployed totalled close to thirty per cent of the workforce.

During these terrible years, the Bridge was known as the Iron Lung, for it kept so many people breathing. It gave work to a fairly constant number of 1,400 men on the site, as well as many thousands more in the steel, cement, sand and stone trades which supplied the immense quantities of materials. To a city bogged down in the demoralisation of worklessness, the great steel pincers nearing each other from the opposing shores must have seemed symbols of prosperity that must one day come again.

The delicate spooky grey of the Bridge is also a legacy of the Depression. When the structure was completed in 1932, grey was the only suitable paint on the market available in sufficient quantities.

The noble massivity of the arch can be best observed from underneath. There also can be seen the two pairs of steel hinge-pins that 'hold up' the arch. Through these pins, each capped with a circular structure, passes the weight of the arch to the foundations deep in the sandstone on which the city stands.

At this point we are but a stroll from one of Sydney's happiest tourist and entertainment centres, Pier One on Walsh Bay. About the time the Tank Stream estuary disappeared under Circular Quay, maritime interest turned to Cockle Bay, or Darling Harbour as it is now known. In Walsh Bay, west of The Rocks, many historic wharves were built, Walker's Wharf taking over the site of a popular swimming bath. Time moved on and so did the big ships, and in 1982 Walker's Wharf, now called Pier One, became a sunburst of lights and bright colours nestling almost under the Bridge. It has everything, including music, free entertainment (at weekends), shops, food, a colonial village, and views that, as Pier One boasts, are good enough to eat.

An unusual place from which to see the Opera House is from the Tarpeian Way. This is the secluded pathway along the top of the high sandstone outcrop on the eastern side of Bennelong Point. Here is the park, very green, with shapely trees, which lies outside the walled gardens of Government

Cedric Emanuel

The Tarpeian Way
now Bennelong Point

House. A glimpse at the vice-regal residence reveals a certain Byronic romanticism. It is battlemented, with sham turrets, massive chimney-stacks, and a good deal of carved stone. Its setting is fantastic, parkland all about, and the roaring Bridge just a stone's throw away.

The Tarpeian Way ends at the head of a wide, graceful flight of stairs which once provided access to Fort Macquarie, the first occupant of this small peninsula. And there is the Opera House, dreamed up in a small village near Copenhagen, paid for by lotteries, sixteen years in the building, one of the wonders of the world. It has been compared to many things, a flower, a swan. But to this writer the Opera House is very much a creature of the sea. To walk inside it is to walk inside an intricate, half-translucent nautilus. Morphology and the computers have composed a world of strange shapes, vast, individual, quite unlike other architecture. And all of extra-ordinary height, all in harmonious dialogue with the sky, the sea, and an almost imperceptible amber that is the sun.

One of the strangest things about this nonesuch of a building is that there is no commemorative plaque that states the name of Jørn Utzon, the primary architect, or the three Australian architects who took over after Utzon's resignation in 1966.

The Opera House was opened by Queen Elizabeth II in October 1973.

from Pinchgut

Pinchgut

Pinchgut Island is about forty metres off Mrs Macquarie's Point. Its correct name is Fort Denison, but who calls it anything but Pinchgut? Naval legend says that its colourful name has nothing to do with convicts or guts, but that the islet was called that by some early surveyor (possibly Captain Hunter, who did the first harbour survey). 'Pinchgut', they say, is a nautical term for the point at which a channel narrows.

Pinchgut didn't always look like that. It was originally a reef with a tall steeple rock, and even a little ruff of vegetation. The Aboriginals loved to fish there, paddling out in their canoes which were, as Captain Watkin Tench said, 'nothing more than a large piece of bark tied up at both ends with vines'. Sometimes these canoes carried little fires, on beds of earth, for cooking the catch immediately.

But after 1797, when a gibbet was erected on Pinchgut and the murderer Morgan hanged there in chains, the Aboriginals took fright and would not go near the place again. There Morgan clanked, blackened and sun-dried, for three years, *pour encourager les autres*.

14

The fort was built during the Russian scare at the time of the Crimean War; the pinnacle was quarried down, and the present structure built of sandstone quarried from Kurraba Point at Neutral Bay. But the guns were never fired in anger. The remaining three 32-pounders were installed in the tower before the top was put on, and cannot be removed without wrecking the fort. Pinchgut was once shelled when a US ship hit it by mistake during target practice in World War II.

Pinchgut is now a museum for cannon and antique matèriel. It can be visited by ferry. These mini-tours are quite unlike anything else and especially fascinating for children. They must be booked by telephoning or writing to the Maritime Services Board.

Pinchgut from Mrs Macquarie's Road

Macquarie Place

THOMAS SUTCLIFFE MORT

Macquarie Place is a shady triangle, irregular in contour, all dips and banks under its enormous Moreton Bay fig trees. Legend says that this space, once just above the beach of Sydney Cove, was a sacred corroboree ground where the two great tribes of the area met for rituals or battles.

But now Macquarie Place is like a queer little village green, very historic, containing at least two of our most important national relics, the severe stone obelisk which Governor Macquarie had erected to mark the starting place for all roads in the colony, and the bower anchor of the *Sirius*.

It's queer to reach up and touch the pocked sun–warm iron of this huge anchor which, aside from the gun which stands nearby, is physically all that we have of the First Fleet. *Sirius* was one of the two escort vessels for the six transports and three supply ships of the First Fleet; she was Captain Phillip's own command. She was a frigate about 30 metres in length, as big as a small ferry.

The *Sirius* first appears in history as 'ye Berwick store-ship'. She was sent to America during the War of Independence, and 'after ye peace, to ye West Indies'. She was re-named *Sirius* after the star which is the southern sky's most magnificent.

On her first voyage as *Sirius* she dropped anchor in Sydney Cove on 26 January 1788. Nine months later, the colony being already starving, the *Sirius* flitted off before the westerlies for Cape Horn and Capetown, where she loaded stores for the afflicted settlers of Sydney. She was therefore the first vessel to sail from Sydney and 'run her easting down'. After loading, she continued to run before the westerlies, circumnavigating the globe in what later were known as the Roaring Forties. Thus she pioneered the great sailing ship route of the later era of commercial sail.

Sirius sailed off again in March 1790, with a cargo of convicts and marines, for Norfolk Island. She was driven on the reef and wrecked, though without loss of life; her anchor was recovered by divers in 1907. The gun was originally removed from the vessel and mounted at Dawes Battery, the site of which is still to be discerned near the southern pylons of the Harbour Bridge. The gun then guarded the Macquarie Lighthouse at South Head for many years.

Governor Macquarie created this tiny park from part of Government House's vegetable garden and bits and pieces of settlers' property which he swapped for other valuable lots of now priceless city real estate. The Place was much larger than it is now, surrounded by orchards and tall flat-faced houses of a style full of the golden light of the eighteenth century. Macquarie intended his formal patch of green to be the hub of administrative Sydney.

It must be remembered that old Government House stood only seventeen metres above highwater mark, on the corner of Bridge and Phillip Streets in their present guise. It was a white-plastered farmhouse amid fields and gardens, and looked over the sparkling harbour and small uninhabited islands.

The first street lamp in Australia stood here in Macquarie Place. Erected in 1826, it burned whale-oil, and was the only one of its kind for more than a year. Three tall graceful old gas lamps, each containing a dim yellow tassel of a pilot light, mark where it stood. These were presented by the Australian Gas Light Company in 1967.

Not far away in Reiby Place stood the modest Georgian cottage of Captain and Mrs Mary Reiby. After her husband's death Mary leased the cottage to the Government and here the Bank of New South Wales (now Westpac) opened for business.

Old drinking fountain

The 'Sirius'
Anchor and Cannon
in Macquarie Place

The Rocks

West of Circular Quay is The Rocks. Though this quaint area has been tidied up, sometimes in the prissiest way, it is still one of the parts of Sydney we love most. An up and down and roundabout village it is now, courts, lanes, stairs, tall houses and low ones. A diabolical place it must have been in its wicked years. People threw up hovels in the shadows of the huge sandstone outcrops; they occupied ledges like seagulls and penguins, or built on top of the rocks like eagles. Flights of steps, goat tracks and children's slides were all that connected them. Sewage ran down the hillsides and piled up against house walls. The place was always a hotbed of typhoid and dysentery as well as poxes big and small. Sailors said that you could hear the roaring of The Rocks a mile out to sea and smell it two miles.

'There were Cheap John shops and shoemakers' hovels and no end of low publick houses. Here might always be seen the British tar and the foreign tar, as incontinently drunk as these noble mariners could desire to be. This is the land of fiddlers and brazen huzzies, of more rum and eternal spree, dancing and singing and brawling and curses and coarse revelry.'

But when Captain Phillip first saw it, Dawes Point must have looked like many another peninsula around Sydney, lying long and narrow in a summer sea, its slopes sparsely

wooded with those rosy-fleshed red gums that live sym-biotically with sandstone, its arid ledges and lintels alight with Christmas bells. The gratified Phillip soon discovered that the characteristic flat sandstone terraces formed a natural quay dipping into five or six fathoms of water.

So this was the site of Hospital Wharf which served the first canvas hospital. George Street began at its door. In its place now stands a grim Victorian police station (no longer used). Above its door is the British lion, holding a police baton in its jaws.

The Rocks was a dangerous, plague-ridden haunt of soldiers and sailors and those who prey on them until well into the twentieth century. At the same time a respectable mari-time and shipside population lived there, pursuing its own industrious life. Whole streets occupied by such people as

Old Cambridge Street,
The Rocks

these still remain, tidied but not tarted up. Such is small Merriman Street, high above Darling Harbour, its houses so plain, so demure, their midget backyards and alleys for the removal of nightsoil still much as they were a century ago when they were occupied by riggers, boatbuilders and stevedores. Close to this spot from 1795 stood one of Jack the Miller's windmills – he is the miller of Miller's Point – but the highest thing to be seen now from the ancient street is the 84-metre Shipping Control Tower. If the visitor strolls through nice little Clyne Reserve at the end of Merriman Street, and goes down the steps into the dogleg lane to the right, Rhoden's Lane, he will see an old smithy that is partly in a sandstone cave. For generations it was worked by the same family.

QANTAS

CLYNE RESERVE
Opened 21st Sep 1981
MERRIMAN STREET
'The Rocks' area.

Cedric Emanuel

Cadman's Cottage

Cadman's Cottage, a lilliputian building beloved of visitors to Sydney, was built for John Cadman in 1815. It is probably the oldest domestic building in Sydney. Cadman, a tiny one-eyed man, was a transportee, and coxs'n of the vice-regal gig in the time of Governor Macquarie. Later he became supervisor of the Rowboat Guard, twelve watermen who watched out for escaping convicts. The Guard appears to have been the ancestor of the Water Police, who later took over Cadman's Cottage, and whose offices and dock are still in the vicinity.

Cadman lived in this cottage during the most notorious period of The Rocks. He retired in 1846 at the age of seventy.

In the 1850s many Chinese settled about here; it was a little Chinatown that gave a living to the many miners who, having worked out their indentures to the Cantonese gold speculators on the Victorian diggings, elected to remain in Australia. Around the lanes and courts of The Rocks they established drinking booths, fantan lottery shops and pak-a-pu establishments. We are told that the fumes of opium hung on the air, accompanied by the peculiar smell of Chinese cooking. As peasant Chinese like to live loudly, the general uproar was such that one visitor commented: 'I feared I should lose my hearing by the deafening noises. Jugglers, dancers and pedlars stopped the thoroughfare, all shouting at the tops of their voices.' An outbreak of smallpox amongst them caused a great scare and led to some cleaning up of The Rocks.

The Argyle Cut and Argyle Place

A spiky dragon's backbone runs through this peninsula, a sandstone ridge which impeded traffic for nearly eighty years. The earliest businessmen recognised the need for a shortcut from the east to the west shores of The Rocks, but it was not until 1843 that work commenced, as part of the construction of Circular Quay. The fearful task was undertaken by Colonel George Barney, the labour being done by convict gangs,

marched down four abreast from Hyde Park Barracks. As stonework was, like roadwork, the severest sentence short of hanging, many of the men were chained.

It was pick and hammer work, slow and arduous. Most of the sandstone removed went to form the Quay seawalls, and the rubble was used as fill on the reclaimed mudflats. Both ends of the Cut are convict work; the middle was excavated by free labour in 1864. It is now spanned by an arch that carries traffic to the Harbour Bridge.

Once through the shadowy precipitous walls of the Cut,

The Hero of Waterloo Hotel
Windmill St and Lower Fort Street, THE ROCKS AREA OF SYDNEY
The oldest hostelry in SYDNEY Est 1802

often running with water, the visitor emerges into the sunny green Englishry of Argyle Place, a true village green. It is benevolently presided over by Holy Trinity Church and faced by dapper old houses on the north. Still lit by gas lamps, Argyle Place is one of the great charmers of Sydney.

The Rocks has many splendid old buildings: hotels such as the Hero of Waterloo on the corner of Windmill Street, which was almost certainly licensed by 1818; some fine bond stores, such as the huge brick Parbury's Bond; oddities, like the isolated house in Kent Street called Noah's Ark, made of mosaic masonry, and standing on an elevated island of stone.

In Lower Fort Street is a lovely terrace of three-storey houses. Though Milton Terrace was built in 1880 when architecture tended to Victorian hyperbole, they are beautifully restrained, with their London-style 'areas' leading presumably to kitchen and offices. Their bedroom windows look

25

Rocks Square SYDNEY

upon the unsurpassed view across the green and under the Bridge, but the noise from the Bridge itself must be insupportable. Beyond them are many other distinctive houses, including probably the finest classical Georgian town house in Sydney, Bligh House, which was built about 1833 for Robert Campbell, son of 'Merchant' Robert Campbell, whose fearless character and extraordinary business acumen finally broke the monopoly trafficking which so besmirches early colonial politics. Robert Campbell the second was a distinguished man in his own right; before his early death in 1859 he was Colonial Treasurer, and also the first representative of

Dwellings Argyle Place
THE ROCKS AREA, SYD
Classified by the National Trust

Cedric Emanuel

Sydney city in the first responsible government. He was also an active campaigner for the cessation of transportation, which duly ceased some ten years before his death.

The Sydney Cove Redevelopment Authority was created in 1970 and has made well over a hundred historic restorations. The area directly around the Argyle Arts Centre is mostly visited by tourists, an open, sunshiny, rather dinky place with many arts and craft shops, and some charming restaurants. Well, it's picturesque, and a fun place, but not really The Rocks. In the midst of all the winsomeness stands, like a blockhouse, the Arts Centre. The oldest part of this formidable structure is along Argyle Street. The lofty arched stone doorway, where the waggons used to rumble over the still-present cobbles, is that of the Old Argyle Bond. Built in 1828, it is where Mary Reiby ran her varied businesses, always accompanied by her servant and bodyguard, a giant Fijian woman named Feefoo.

Across the courtyard is a newer bond store built in 1881. But it too has an atmosphere of older and sterner days. Its windows are barred, its adzed ironbark beams look as if they will outlast the Pyramids. It is a fortress, and no wonder, as it was a spirits bond store.

The Garrison Church

Holy Trinity Church, or as it is familiarly known, the Garrison Church, is a constantly used, not too well-endowed, parish church, Gothic in style, with flags and regimental shields on the pillars, a wine-glass pulpit of red cedar, and a delightful east window, glittering like Celtic enamel in the gentle gloom.

It stands east of Argyle Place in The Rocks.

The foundation stone was laid in 1840, and the church itself built from stone quarried out of the cliff behind. It was built by free men, but convicts carted away the rubble and did other heavy labour. It became the first official Garrison Church of the colony. It is easy to imagine these dark pews filled with redcoats, marched up from Dawes Battery for morning prayer. In spite of many generous gifts, Holy Trinity was not rich, and for some time its windows were made of oiled canvas, mediaeval style. By 1878 the church had been enlarged and in some ways altered by the architect Edmund Blacket, but before this the eastern window was donated by book-collector David Scott Mitchell's mother in memory of her parents.

Observatory Park

Observatory Park is elevated on a high sandstone bluff that was carved away into a cliff at the western side. There's a tall iron fence along the edge of this cliff, a fortress-like palisade, and through it you may look down into the backyards of the Kent Street houses and inspect the poinsettias, frangipani and washing.

There is a surfy sound of traffic from the spider-grey Bridge, and a great view all around, sometimes so bright that the water dazzles, and there's a faint down of light around the three TV masts on the northern shore. Other times smog works its magic, and the whole world is seen through an opal haze, faint and flower-tinted, so that docks, ships' masts, wooded headlands, monster buildings with cranes scissoring the sky, even the diabolic BP tanks, assume the mysterious beauty of a mirage.

The older buildings of the Observatory are of rain-stained stone. They have low, faded green domes, and look their age. Young Lieutenant Dawes built a tiny tinpot observatory close to his Battery, down there on Dawes Point. At that time this hill was called Flagstaff Hill. Later Fort Phillip was built here,

Headquarters of The National Trust and the S.H. Ervin Museum and Art Gallery

At the Sydney Observatory

and still later an important windmill was erected upon the highest point.

The present Observatory was erected in 1855. In the Observatory are preserved some of the earliest astronomical instruments brought to Australia, including those used by Governor Brisbane in his private observatory at Parramatta.

Close to the Observatory site stood Fort Phillip, a pretentious hexagonal building designed to glare out to sea and frighten off French and American invaders, the bogeys of the 1810s and 1820s. Within very few years it fell into disuse. Governor Macquarie's Military Hospital, built a little to the south of the Fort, was completed in Waterloo year, 1815. It was designed by John Watts, who had architectural training before he joined the army during the Napoleonic Wars. Later he became Macquarie's aide-de-camp.

Its conversion to a national Model School in 1849 (at three pence per pupil) was the beginning of an outstanding academic history which did not end until the Girls' High School closed at the end of 1974. The demolition of many school buildings has permitted much of the original Watts design to emerge. This graceful structure is now the National Trust Headquarters and also houses the S.H. Ervin Museum and Art Gallery.

the Agar Steps
from Observatory Hill
Cedric Emanuel 1983

Hangman's Hill

There's something very disturbing about Essex Street. It's sunny, very steep, leaping to each of its levels with flights of worn stone steps. This is Hangman's Hill.

The public gallows dominated this end of the town until 1804 when they were moved to the corner of present Park and Castlereagh Streets. Being returned to Essex Street, they stood here from 1820 until 1841 when the new gaol was built at Darlinghurst.

Now there is nothing but sunlight and silence in Essex Street. In its fatal days it must have been muddy, for it drained the rocky steeps of Cambridge and Gloucester Streets. On the present level between Gloucester and Harrington Streets, in

Essex Street
'The Rocks'

the middle of the road, is a weird little grassy plot on a built-up embankment of random freestone. Two trees grow where the gallows stood, one a palm as tall as a ship's mast.

All the stonework connected with this grassy plot looks very old. Beside it run archaic gutters, stones tipped to a point, European style.

Well, some curious people were turned off here, including in 1803 the wretched Joseph Samuels, 'the man they couldn't hang'. Samuels was one of four petty criminals accused of robbery and the subsequent murder of a constable who chased them. Before an immense and hostile crowd, aghast at what must have been a fearful scene, the executioners endeavoured to do their duty though the rope suspending the unfortunate Samuels broke three times. Governor King instantly reprieved the unfortunate victim.

Samuels was always slightly queer in the attic afterwards. His end was odd. He was one of eight convicts who eloped from the Hunter River coalmines in 1806, stole a boat, and pushed out to sea. They were last seen driving before a storm along the north coast and were never heard of again.

It is difficult for us to understand authority's insistence on public executions in centuries gone by. The immense public interest, which seems to us ghoulish and brutalised, was accepted as natural, indeed praiseworthy. The Golden Cob, a quite respectable pub in Essex Street, had a special viewing window for its aficionados of hanging.

35

The General Post Office

Like many other High Victorian buildings in Sydney, the General Post Office was planned to be completed in time to celebrate the gala centennial of the colony in 1888. It is the third of its kind. The first, Isaac Nichols's house near the Quay, became a Chinese warehouse. The second was pillared and portico'ed, and situated in George Street between King and Hunter Streets.

At this time Martin Place did not exist. The centre of the city was a perfect maze of tiny lanes, unpaved, running with either rain or sewage. Between tall handsome buildings were dreadful courts like the bottoms of chimneys, full of 'pigeons, goats, dirt and washing'. Sometimes there was only one standpipe to provide the entire lane or court with water. In fact, the area was a splendid example of the extraordinary way the Victorians lived, wealth and grandeur cheek by jowl with crime, filth and misery. Foxlow Lane, which for decades sent city Health Officers into fits, ran just where the steps of the GPO lie now. It was a kind of cesspit constantly seething with smallpox and bubonic plague.

Most of the property bought for the GPO and Martin Place belonged to the stepdaughters of the fabulous Sam Terry, the miser millionaire, the one with the gold bracelets and no socks.

The GPO is impressive but inert. It reclines rather than stands on its important site. Its architect and builder was James Barnet, who is shown on one of the sculptured inserts as a Jovian person with waving beard and extravagant pompadour. Poor dear, he was in fact totally bald.

The experienced and able Barnet became Colonial Architect in 1865. He designed many public buildings, including the drear khaki Museum in College Street, and, to make up

Cedric Emanuel

for that, the enchanting Mortuary Railway Station at Redfern.

After twenty-eight years a-building, the General Post Office was completed in 1887. It had the first electric lifts in Sydney and all kinds of trendy telegraphic equipment. People wrote songs about it, its handsome clock tower, and the wealth of sculpture lavished upon its façade. It was the dignified voice, they fancied, of an imperial nation, and perhaps it was.

The GPO now looks out, dignified as ever, upon a Martin Place that has, one feels, reached a pause in its evolution. A rosy-paved pedestrian plaza from Macquarie to George Streets, it has become a lively gathering-place for Sydney-siders. The Eastern Suburbs Railway station is discreet, the fountains do not blow water over passers-by, there is always something interesting going on in the entertainment amphitheatre. The graceful slope to the east is dominated by a silver monolith, the Dobell Memorial Sculpture.

The glittering spire (by the sculptor Bert Flugelman) occasionally frets the citizenry, who cry 'science fiction' and see in it little reference to the richly earthy quality of William Dobell's art. Well, it may give only an enigmatic hint about Dobell, but as it leaps from its greenery, going straight for the sky, surely it is symbolic of Martin Place.

Flower Stall

Mysteriously this location has always been the heart of the city. On both sides the present spacious forum dips down into, and crosses, the Vale of Sydney. Here in a bird-haunted wood, the stream of fresh water stealing silently down to the sea, the first trees were felled, the first huts built. Close to the east bank of that now darkened, imprisoned stream stands the Dobell Memorial, and this writer for one calls it well-placed.

The Dobell Memorial Sculpture Oct. 1979

Lloyd Rees Fountain

Mrs Macquarie's Road

Mrs Macquarie's Road is about five kilometres long; it was built by her husband, from Old Government House to the point named for her. Here she liked to sit. It now runs right around the west side of Woolloomooloo Bay in a long loop, but the portion that connected with Bridge Street seems to have been swallowed up by the Cahill Expressway.

Lachlan Macquarie was born in 1761 on the island of Ulva in the Inner Hebrides in Scotland in a freakish January in which 'birds nested and strawberries ripened'. On another January in 1810, when he was nearly 49, he arrived in Sydney to take control of the colony from the mutinous leaders of the Rum Rebellion who had deposed Governor Bligh. Macquarie was a man of long military experience, mostly in India. He had typical Scots family pride, though that family had long been ruinously poor.

His wife was a Jane Austen lady, slight, pretty and accomplished, the compleat gentlewoman, privately endowed with considerable pawky humour. She was a woman of Napoleonic times, for a good deal of her life had been lived under the shadow of impending French invasion.

Mrs Macquarie came into a ramshackle town where all the windows were tiny-paned because the colonists couldn't get glass of any other size, and the roof shingles were painted blue because that was the colour paint that could be purchased. A third of the population wore military or naval uniform, and the rest, if female, were in tattered brown serge jackets and petticoats, and if male, in summer-issue dark frocks over canvas pantaloons. The women of Mrs Macquarie's own social class were mostly disagreeable proud ladies who were against everyone and everything. Everyone who could write wrote poisonous, tattling, malcontent letters to influential friends at Home.

No wonder Mrs Macquarie went for long walks, usually

accompanied only by an aide-de-camp, and George, the Governor's black servant, whom he and his first wife, the consumptive Jane, had bought as a child in India for 85 rupees. George was the Governor's faithful companion all his life, and was present at his death in miserable lodgings in London. Although the British Government treated Macquarie with shameful stinginess, and Elizabeth was poorly off after his death, she set up the Macquarie Trust to look after the descendants of George, who married whilst in Sydney.

STEPHEN ST

Little Stone House
(Formerly Boot maker)
Woolloomooloo
Cedric Emanuel

Historic Houses
CAMP COVE
Cedric Emanuel

Merriman Street 'The Rocks' Sydney

Kent St, THE ROCKS
Adrie Emanuel

Sydney Harbour
from Gibson's Beach.
WATSON'S BAY

Cedric Emanuel

The Alice Lee Reserve
Barton Street
GLEBE
Cedric Emanuel

ST JAMES ROAD

Cedric Emanuel

Old Sydney
St James Road at Elizabeth St.

Victoria Terrace
'THE ROCKS' SYDNEY
Cedric Emanuel

One of the vanishing
corner grocer shops

Glebe Notes Cedric Emanuel

Former SHIPWRIGHTS ARMS HOTEL
The ROCKS area of Sydney
Cedric Emanuel

'Coal and Candle – Pittwater'
Cedric Emanuel

The old Mortuary Station
CENTRAL STATION.
James Barnet 1869
Cedric Emanuel 1982

ELKINS
FIB FEBRUARY 6th
AGED 3 YEARS

MATTHEWS — WINDSOR

The Art Gallery

When reconstruction began on the Art Gallery in the early 1970s, the Government Architect intimated that the aim was to double the space, but to be polite to the old section. The old section, weightily Roman and constructed in a peculiarly dead brown Pyrmont sandstone, is what confronts us. It scarcely deserves respect, being one of the Victorian architect Horbury Hunt's more derivative designs. How could he have produced this khaki railway station, a man so eccentric and original, who designed his bicycle to double as both steed and fully-fitted architect's studio?

The new Gallery provides five storeys behind this façade; it begins directly behind the massive arches of the lobby, in a curiously tacked-on style. It is air-conditioned, fitted with highly sophisticated security systems, provided with ample workshops, two kilometres of racking space, restaurant, exhibition rooms, a sculpture courtyard, administrative offices and so on. All of these were exasperatingly lacking in the old Gallery. The architecture of the new block has been described as New Brutalism; flea-bitten concrete, lofty roofs and ceilings with no ornamentation, pebble colours, grey, white, beige. Yet there's wonderful space, airiness, and superb lighting. At the corners lofty glass panels let in a troll's cityscape, the highrise buildings of King's Cross and Darlinghurst, leaned-upon by rainclouds; rusty ships, dull sleeping water of Woolloomooloo Bay.

The Gallery is celebrated for its collections of Australian paintings, primitive Pacific art, and a rich display of Victorian genre 'wrinklies'.

RECLINING FIGURE
Henry Moore 1980
(ENGLISH 1898)

The Domain

Though history says that the Domain was opened to the public in 1888, it seems to have been free to them, perhaps on certain days, for long before that. B.C. Peck in his *Recollections of Sydney*, written about 1848, mentions Monday afternoons, between four and five, when the band of the 99th Regiment played lively polkas for the fashionables and the unfashionables. He describes charmingly dressed ladies, in their splendid carriages, 'with favoured gentlemen leaning on the doors to chat with these admired ones'. The unfashionable are 'settlers from the interior whose immense beards and moustaches, monkey jackets and cabbage-tree hats give them a Robinson Crusoe-like appearance'.

Some curious things have happened in the Domain. In 1820 there was a procession round and round, and then west to St Phillip's behind a band playing the Dead March from *Saul*, 'All, wearing crape and suitably composed expressions, from the highest to the lowest, marched lamenting'. This was to mark the death of George III.

There were colossal gatherings to protest against conscription in 1917, and even greater ones (judged in excess of 100,000) to protest against the Governor's dismissal of Premier J.D. Lang in 1931. 'From north, south, east and west they came, until it seemed that the whole of the city and suburbs had taken to the roads that led to the Domain . . . "Are the people of New South Wales going to say they will give a nominee governor powers which the British people took away from a hereditary king 300 years ago?" asked Mr Lang. With a response that could be heard through the wide expanse of the Domain, the citizens shouted their most pronounced "No!".'

On Sunday the Domain is the battleground of the public speakers, still noisily debating the same old issues of religion and politics, daylight-saving and Women's Lib.

BURNS
1759-1796

Domain entrance and Lodge

St Mary's Cathedral

Standing between the Domain and Hyde Park, St Mary's position can scarcely be bettered. Church authorities must be grateful that Governor Macquarie did not heed the plaintive cries with which the original land grant was received by Father Joseph Therry, the builder of the first St Mary's. He had his heart set on a more fashionable site, on The Rocks ridge, but instead found himself cheek by jowl with convict barracks, hospital and racecourse.

Macquarie (a Mason and Protestant) laid the foundation stone, and slowly, over a period of thirty years, the huge Gothic church arose. It was paid for by the city's Catholics, mostly ex-convicts and poor Irish migrants, and completed in 1837. Twenty-eight years later, in 1865, St Mary's burned to the ground. A third brick building was demolished when the present cathedral was opened in 1882.

It is an astonishing church for what was then a tiny remote city; built in thirteenth-century style and much larger than many of the mediaeval European cathedrals. Its length is 100 metres, its width 40 metres and its height more than 45 metres. Its nave is 30 metres high. It is said that, when the cathedral was built, nothing of its style and magnitude had been attempted for two centuries. Certainly nothing resembling it is likely to be built again.

St Mary's possesses one of Sydney's ten belltowers.

Whilst St Mary's tradition and beauty make it worth visiting, I find the crypt the more unusual and fascinating feature. In the floor of the crypt Australia's largest mosaic (some 700 square metres) makes a dazzling pathway to the sanctuary. The work is done in the angelically pure blues, greens and scarlets of antique Celtic enamelwork. One is dumbfounded that such a treasure should be in a little-visited crypt, though the latter is, in truth, as vast and impressive as many a church. Upon closer scrutiny one distinguishes in this jewelled stone a chain of motifs depicting the six days of Creation; these are surrounded by the fantastic knots, angles and Daedalian coils of archaic Irish art.

This mosaic was the work of 'Mr Peter' as he was called during the sixteen years he devoted to it. Peter Melocco, senior member of the mosaic and terrazzo firm, Melocco Bros, came to Australia in 1908. The slight, perfectionist Italian supervised many other decorative works about the cathedral, including the baptistry and font, but the crypt floor was his masterpiece and personal concern, much of the work being done at his own cost. It was completed in 1961, the year of Peter Melocco's death. In 1972 this unpublicised work of art was given the top award by the National Terrazzo and Mosaic Association of the United States.

Hyde Park

The Busby Bore

This delightful city greenspace was once part of the Sydney Common, which really meant the bushranger-haunted swamps and scrub between the struggling village on the Harbour and the remote outpost of Botany Bay. The colonial breast, being British, had long pined for a racecourse so, when Macquarie came, a portion of the common was designated Hyde Park and turned over to the Governor's regiment, the 73rd. The troops cleared the common, grubbed out the stumps, and laid out a 10-furlong course. The first race meeting, October 1810, was organised by the officers, and a grandstand was erected almost opposite David Jones's display windows on Elizabeth Street.

It is said that at this historic spring meeting – the first in Australia – the horses ran clockwise, thus founding the New South Wales and Queensland tradition. In other States they run anti-clockwise.

49

The Archibald Fountain

The Anzac Memorial

50

The Walker Fountain

Hyde Park was Sydney's racecourse until the late 1820s; it then became the Cricket Ground. Until the 1850s its reputation was rowdy; sporting taverns sprang up along Elizabeth and Park Streets; private sports meetings, wrestling and boxing matches were held on holidays; circus and sideshow proprietors set up their booths where they willed. Hyde Park also saw Sydney's first zoo, curiously organised by the Museum. This was in 1849.

Nowadays grand massy trees offer sylvan corners to lunchtime dawdlers, chess and draught-players sit in deep concentration amongst art exhibitions, folk-dancing, brass-band concerts and other gentle urban entertainments. Rainbows halo the Archibald Memorial Fountain, a rather stately classical group of figures symbolising the goodies amongst the national virtues and the Olympian personnel. It was donated by J.F. Archibald, editor, art-lover and nationalist, who died in 1919. The fountain was handed over to the people of Sydney in 1933.

The queer little fountain like a succession of cement soup plates near the north-west corner of Hyde Park is a memorial to Sydney's first water supply, the Busby Bore. There are quite a number of things under Hyde Park, such as an air-raid shelter, but the most historic is this terrible stone tunnel which brought water several kilometres from the Lachlan Swamps, now Centennial Park. The convicts who toiled during the ten-year period of construction could not stand upright in the tunnel. The Busby Bore served Sydney for some decades. The watercarts filled up at a standpipe at the corner of Park Street, where the Ladies' Rest Rooms now stand.

51

The inscription on the statue reads:

SHAKESPERE
1564 · 1616

PRESENTED TO
THE CITY OF SYDNEY
BY
HENRY GULLETT
AUGUST 1914

OUR REVELS NOW ARE ENDED, THESE OUR ACTORS
AS I FORETOLD YOU, WERE ALL SPIRITS, AND
ARE MELTED INTO AIR, INTO THIN AIR:
AND LIKE THE BASELESS FABRIC OF THIS VISION
THE CLOUD-CAPP'D TOWERS, THE GORGEOUS PALACES,
THE SOLEMN TEMPLES, THE GREAT GLOBE ITSELF
YEA, ALL WHICH IT INHERIT, SHALL DISSOLVE
AND LIKE THIS INSUBSTANTIAL PAGENT FADED
LEAVE NOT A RACK BEHIND, WE ARE SUCH STUFF
AS DREAMS ARE MADE ON! AND OUR LITTLE LIFE
IS ROUNDED WITH A SLEEP.

The State Library

Though Sydney people almost invariably refer to this splendid block as 'the Mitchell', it is in fact the State Library, housing in the same building the Shakespeare Memorial Library, and the Mitchell and Dixson Libraries and Galleries.

Its site, which offers a pastoral view of trees, meadowland and Harbour, had been originally reserved for a new Parliament House. The lobby is admirable, lofty and uncluttered, its floor inlaid by the Sydney craftsmen, Melocco Bros, with Abel Tasman's seventeenth-century map of New Holland.

The northwest wing of the Library was first and specifically built to house the priceless Australiana collection given to the library by the wealthy recluse, David Scott Mitchell. The original total bequests from Mitchell, comprising 61,000 items (books, maps, manuscripts, pictures) together with a fund for their housing and upkeep, have been so added to by purchases, legacies and gifts from other collectors that we have here the world's greatest collection of Australiana. Amongst the Mitchell treasures are the original journals of James Cook and Joseph Banks, Captain Bligh's *Bounty* log, and valuable manuscripts relating to the 17th century explorations of Abel Tasman, de Quiros and Torres.

The Sydney legend is that D.S. Mitchell was early crossed in love and became a recluse. His quaintly respectable figure, clad in sober garments with a bowler at one end and black elastic-sided boots at the other, was familiar to booksellers for some decades. On Monday mornings he went his rounds most punctually, and was known to the drivers of the cabs he hired as 'Old Four Hours'.

Mitchell, like all book collectors, suffered torments when a rival scooped some treasure of Australiana from under his nose. Fortunately, he was able to outbid most of them. Ardently desiring the original Joseph Banks diaries, he bought the entire library of their owner, Alfred Lee, for seven thousand pounds, a fortune in the early years of this century.

Another shy bachelor collector, Sir William Dixson, collected objects of Pacific interest; maps, coins, portraits and memorabilia of the early settlement. Three of the stained-glass windows and the handsome bronze doors of the Library are also a gift from Sir William Dixson.

By an extraordinary stroke of good fortune Dixson, who died in 1952, took up collecting almost where David Scott Mitchell left off. Between them they covered very nearly a century of collecting. Sir William's bequest to the Library included more than 20,000 items, as well as investments worth more than a quarter of a million dollars. The income is devoted to the reproduction of historical manuscripts, translations of non-English books of Australian interest, and the reprinting of rare books.

Royal Botanic Gardens
from the State Library 1983

Cedric Emanuel

Hyde Park Barracks, Queen's Square 1817.

Hyde Park Barracks

The Hyde Park Barracks is a distinguished building that shouts 'Greenway' in every line. A convict appointed by Governor Macquarie to be the Government's Civil Architect, Greenway's bigness of scale, rarest excellence in his art, is nowhere expressed better than in this Macquarie structure.

Until the early 1980s the Barracks was treated with outrageous disregard for its beauty and historicity. Of the original complex, only the centre building, a portion of a cell block, the gate piers, and some fragments of wall remain. This central building, like the vanished portions constructed of soft red brick, bears the well-known triangular pediment, ornamented by a crown, a large clock, and the words 'L. Macquarie, Esq., Governor 1817'.

Francis Greenway, who wore ill-luck like an old shirt, swiftly fell into disfavour after the departure of Macquarie. The things that happened to that man! His eldest son was drowned, dogs bit him, footpads bashed and robbed him, his wife died, he was driven from his house. Ruined and miserable, he died in 1837 in East Maitland, and is buried in a grave now forgotten.

Folklore says that Greenway died of a broken heart, and we may believe it. Yet, as we look at this simple fragment of a building, his great feeling for beauty strikes us anew. On a poorhouse budget, he achieved not only his usual excellence of proportion, but graceful ornamentation within the limits of the few materials available to him – the pretty red rubbing bricks of the arches and window heads, the base course and string-courses of finely-worked stone.

When Macquarie came to Sydney, the inhumane law was that the felons were fed and employed by Government, but not lodged. Many were assigned as servants and lived in; others with some small financial resources built slab shanties. But the homeless, after their day's work was finished, slept in the open or begged for the privilege of sleeping in someone's henhouse or stable. The ill-lit or pitch-dark streets, thus inhabited by crowds of vagrant, 'depraved creatures that knew not God nor the patronage of Mammon', were nightly the scene of robberies, brawls and murders.

Hyde Park Barracks was designed as a male convict dormitory. It was built in two years, and from 1822 was occupied by up to 900 convicts. Although the men were fed, clothed and sheltered, they didn't like communal living, and it became a privilege to sleep out. These were men of fair character, and they were called out-of-barrack men.

There were twelve large airy wards, each in charge of a watchman. The men slept in hammocks, and were called at sunrise to a nourishing breakfast of porridge, which they hated. We are told 'a generous quantity generally remains'. They were, after a while, put into a dreary uniform of yellowish grey canvas, branded HPB from the place of their origin, and marched off to work, some of the recalcitrant wearing leg-irons. At twelve they marched back to dine on a meal 'not insufficient to dispel the quirks and crochets of a moderate appetite'. The dish was a sort of soupy stew of salt beef and vegetables, served in small tubs, one for each mess of six men. The men had an hour for lunch, worked the rest of the afternoon until sunset, and retired to rest at six.

Macquarie reported that street robberies and fights dropped to one-tenth shortly after the Barracks were occupied.

In 1848, as a result of constant complaints from Sydney citizens about the now notorious convict barracks in the middle of the town, the remaining male convicts were transferred to Cockatoo Island. The building then entered upon the most picturesque part of its existence, when it was a staging-camp for thousands of newly-arrived immigrants.

For much of this century the Barracks became the official slum described earlier. But in the 1980s restoration work began. The shameful jerry-built additions were cast down, the austere elegance of Greenway's original design emerged. Like its near neighbour the old Mint, the Hyde Park Barracks has become a museum. Aside from presenting a re-creation of the convict barracks, its speciality will be the collection and display of the social history of New South Wales.

This building looks its best when the western sun strikes between tall buildings. Then the upper air, its pollution visible, is full of spinning detritus like disintegrating tinsel, and the faintly-veiled light lies upon the Hyde Park Barracks like the reflection from a fire.

It is a magnificent memorial to that lost unhappy man, Francis Greenway.

Parliament House

The more graceful remnants of the Rum Hospital stay in use. The north wing has been Parliament House since 1829. Of course the Legislative Council, in those days, was non-elective. In 1843 the colonial architect, Mortimer Lewis, designed the unimpressive north addition. The south adit, much more interesting, is one of the iron prefabs often used in early Sydney.

There have been many attempts to house more fittingly the Australian Mother of Parliaments. But somehow Parliament has gone on sitting in this hugger-mugger of Georgian, early Victorian and later structures. It has seen every hard-fought step towards self-government since 1823 when the Governor was 'an unhampered tyrant, responsible only to the Home Office in a city (London) unknown to the majority and half-forgotten by the rest'.

The building has resounded to the roars of rough, tough politicians and their hatchetmen in those robust days when gentlemen did not mince words; when, to quote one of them, 'they stood face to face like men and did not crawl about the face of the earth like those who now beslime it with their unsightly and unclean carcases . . .' This was Henry Parkes in 1880.

Cedric Emanuel

N.S.W. State Parliament House.

Sydney Hospital

Sydney Hospital's façade, sullen and unconfident, displays all the faults of degenerated Victorian style. Its position, open to the dirt and noise of a major thoroughfare, is poor. The Hospital, which began work in 1894, was subjected to severe upheavals in the early 1980s, when a large number of its beds, in a kind of Government Diaspora, were 'given' to distant suburban hospitals.

The Hospital occupies the site of the centre block of the historic Rum Hospital, of which the north and south wings still exist. That on the left is used as the State Parliament House; except for the middle section, the bold gauntness of the original building has been sicklied o'er by additions. The wing to the right of the Sydney Hospital, familiarly called the old Mint, is used as a museum of Australian decorative arts. It retains the simplicity of the original Rum Hospital, which in early sketches shows up on the eastern ridge as bare as a picked bone.

Governor Macquarie had always wanted a capacious hospital. The existing hospitals at Parramatta and at George Street North were overcrowded and dilapidated. They were occupied not only by the sick but by old or infirm convicts, for whom the Government was responsible. The urgency of the matter eventually caused the Governor to revert to the evil custom of pre-Rum Rebellion days when almost everything was paid for either by spirits or the grant of monopolies for its import and sale. Foolishly, one feels, Macquarie agreed to the conditions of a triumvirate who submitted a tender for the hospital's erection.

Surgeon D'Arcy Wentworth (W.C. Wentworth's father), Garnham Blaxcell and Alexander Riley were given a rum monopoly for three years, during which time they were permitted to import 45,000 gallons. They were allowed the free use of twenty convicts and twenty working bullocks, and rations for both. It is said that each contractor made £10,000 from this deal.

In 1816 the patients were transferred from the decaying building in George Street North. D'Arcy Wentworth was Surgeon-in-Charge for three years. During this time 'a gloomy disorder prevailed, and hell itself could not hope to rival the melancholy torments of the helpless sick'.

The kitchen was the deadhouse. (It was said that when the building was eventually demolished in the 1870s, many bones, possibly of amputated limbs, were found buried beneath its floor.) The nurses and wardsmen were convicts, 'depraved and drunken, delinquent ravenous wretches that stole the patients' food and peddled the very rags away from them'. These ghouls were locked up with the patients in the wards from sunset to sunrise.

Treatment was of the most ruthless: bleeding, purgatives, starvings, cold douches. Yet some survived to be convalescent, and they joined the merry horde of sheet-snatchers and ration-floggers.

In 1868 began a new era. Miss Lucy Osburn headed the six Nightingale nurses who arrived in answer to Henry Parkes's request to the invalid but still vigorous Miss Nightingale. Matron Osburn, a dark-haired pretty creature, looked upon nursing as the highest female employment. She was, we are told, 'an exceptional woman, well-read, having an absolute fascination of manner and a most indomitable will'.

The present Hospital was declared open by Sir George Dibbs in 1894. It still incorporated several of the jerry-built buildings of earlier days, and could accommodate somewhat more than 250 in-patients. The resident medical staff that year was four.

Sydney Hospital MACQUARIE STREET

The Mint Building

The Mint Building is the southern wing of the old Rum Hospital. Though it was used for a number of other purposes, it was for seventy-one years the New South Wales branch of the Royal Mint, and in its first three years minted more than £5,000,000 worth of sovereigns from the State's newly found goldmines. The name has stuck and suits the building very well.

In the early 1980s the battered old building was restored. It is now a perfect picture, painted in authentic old-colonial hues of brownish rose, trimmed with sour cream. Long shallow staircases, graceful arches and lofty windows are a background for thousands of quaint Australian treasures. For the old Mint Building is now a museum for decorative art, a companion for its neighbour, the Hyde Park Barracks, which will display the social history of New South Wales.

The 'old' Mint restored

High Victoriana

Town Hall

The Town Hall is one of a stately group of High Victorian buildings which includes St Andrew's Cathedral, the Gresham Hotel, the Queen Victoria Building, and the former Bank of New South Wales on the corner of Bathurst Street. These tiddlywinked old pets are superbly contrasted with the strong vertical lines of the near-by Water Board Building. The Cathedral, which for nearly a century was semi-submerged in a clutter of glum church edifices, now keeps company with the Town Hall in the rather windy but elegant Sydney Square.

According to its own public relations department, the Town Hall is one of the noblest civic structures south of the Line.

Civic structure indeed. From the air it looks like a thumping great hippo. Even walking around it you are uneasily aware of dropsical protuberances and swellings which shouldn't be there; they offend an eye perhaps put out by the gaunt pale simplicities of Georgian style.

The Town Hall, because of certain scandals and charges of corruption during its construction, has been called the graveyard of reputations. It is in fact built on a graveyard, Sydney's second, which was in use from 1793.

Governor Macquarie built a high brick wall around it and on maps after 1820, it is marked FULL. It must have been a great eyesore; half-wild pigs roamed amongst the graves, and it was a haunt of bad characters who lit picnic fires with paling fences and bivouacked within broken vaults. The *Gazette* thundered: 'Dastard must be the living spirit that would thus pollute the mansions of the dead with wanton and unprofitable crime . . .'

Being municipal property, the derelict Old Burial Ground was resumed in 1869, and the bones of the earliest settlers, both free and unfree, were carted out to the Sandhills (Devonshire Street Cemetery) from which they were moved once more when Central Railway took over. It is thought that a number of coffins remain beneath the Town Hall.

The foundation stone of the Town Hall was laid by the Duke of Edinburgh, that royal 'Affie' whom some earnest anarchist endeavoured to bowl over at the picnic races at Clontarf in 1868.

It is indeed a huge structure, occupying nearly a hectare, its external dimensions being 95 metres long, 57 metres wide, and its height to the main parapet 21 metres. The tower is close to 55 metres high, and there is a flagpole on top of that. The architectural style is pure Bondi Renaissance, and if you are a collector of columns you can find every variety known to the mind of man.

The Centennial Hall, also, with its impressive galleries and spacious orchestral platform is enriched with an unusual ceiling of panelled and coffered zinc. Metal in fact is used surprisingly often around this Victorian building; the striking large domes on the exterior roof are of polished steel and some of the clerestory windows have sashes of wrought-iron.

The Centennial Hall, before the erection of the Opera House, was the scene of almost all important concerts. It can seat 2,535 persons and it is supposed to be the world's largest entertainments hall built in conjunction with a city hall. However, its acoustic properties are often carped at.

St. Andrews Cathedral & Town Hall, Sydney

Queen Victoria Building

The Town Hall almost avoided the perverse Sydney tradition which decrees that all large works must be carried through in times of utmost economic crisis. For example the Harbour Bridge arose in a period of unparalleled unemployment, hardship and despair.

St Andrew's Cathedral's history follows this pattern. Building commenced in 1837. Two years later the finances of colonial Anglicanism tottered before the onslaught of the Great Depression of the 1840s. An editorial of 1844 commented 'Everything is struck with a kind of paralysis. The banks narrowed their discounts and smash went the whole of our prosperity . . . and vanished like the dream of a drunkard.'

In 1846 work on the Cathedral recommenced under the direction of Edmund Blacket, a delightful young man, gifted musician, sculptor and painter as well as architect. He concluded his work for the great church in 1874.

St Andrew's is a tall thin building with much dark timber and carving and massy pillars like close-knit banyan trees. It has the military atmosphere of most Anglican establishments, with many tattered flags and a flock of regimental crests. It is very much a church, comforting and enfolding, always with people praying or meditating within. Indeed it is the oldest cathedral in Australia, never having ceased to serve its worshippers. Beautiful in the daylight, behind its lacy jacarandas, it is more so at night, being illuminated with great skill. Massive blocks of darkness support faintly-limned arches, the quaint tick-tack-toed spires beloved of Blacket spindle imperceptibly into the night sky.

The depression of the 1890s rivalled that of the 1840s. 'Ruin, famine and dread suicide stalk the land' said a newspaper leader. So the City Council bought from the State Government the huge block from Druitt Street to Market Street and launched into the construction of a building so large it looks like something conjured up by Aladdin's lamp.

The Queen Victoria Building is a majestic example of its kind. Like the Town Hall, it is ornate, but whereas the former is prinked, pranked and bedizened, the ornaments worn by the Queen Victoria Building are as unaffectedly splendid as those of a moth or a seashell.

The dimensions, which stupefied little Victorian Sydney, are still impressive today. The length is 186 metres. Here, from Market to Druitt Streets, roofed with an elaborate barrel-vault of glass, once ran the Avenue, an arcade 10 metres wide and 20 metres high. It had the prettiest tesselated marble pavement (now mostly hidden by timber flooring), arches, upper galleries, and handsome little footbridges connecting floor to floor. Along this arcade were fifty-eight shops and coffee houses, and at the Druitt Street end was a hotel with fifty-seven bedrooms and elegant public and private restaurants.

The Queen Victoria was built as a market building. On this site there had always been a market, in long rows of sheds. In 1828 the produce was rural, homemade butter, green forage, sucking pigs. By 1846 local wines were on sale, also flying-foxes, emus, and colonial tobacco. In the taproom where you could drink 'rum slightly qualified with water', it is said that Henry Parkes, then a penniless immigrant but later the Founding Father of Federation, made his first political speech.

In its dazzling romanticism the Queen Victoria Building is the symbol of the innocent pomp of an age whose prime article of faith was that the Empire would last forever, and that the dignity of Great Britain must be upheld on Australia's coral strand.

The Great Synagogue

The Great Synagogue, sumptuously Eastern, looks across to the greensward and the cascading flower baskets of Hyde Park.

The wheel-window repeats the design of the magnificent tall wrought-iron gates and is considered one of the finest in Sydney. Under the broad shallow porch arches, all in opulently-worked stone, one can best see the details of that portico which architect Thomas Rowe considered the 'most gorgeous and ornate' he had ever designed.

The Jewish community, which in Sydney numbers about twenty-eight thousand, began with the First Fleet, when James Larra arrived on the *Scarborough*. He became a prosperous hotel keeper in Parramatta. In 1817 twenty members of the Jewish faith formed a society for the burial of their dead, and a small portion of the Town Hall graveyard was given over to them. Divine worship according to the Hebrew rites was officially performed in 1828, and the first Rabbi arrived in 1830.

The Great Synagogue
ELIZABETH ST. SYDNEY

Cedric Emanuel

Mortuary Station

All Saints', Ainslie

Like every other city in the world in the second half of last century, Sydney was devoted to extravagant mourning, undertakers in tall hats, baroque funerals and funeral trappings, and graveyards full of every funerary conceit from weeping angels to shattered harps.

An enchanting memorial to this spectacular grief is the Regent Street Mortuary Station. It was designed by James Barnet, Colonial Architect, in 1869 and is quaintly grotesque, with cloister-like carved sandstone arches and impressive columns. In the days of its prime the Mortuary Station was close to the then Sydney terminal, Redfern. (See the last page of the colour section.)

A funeral cortège would arrive under the arches. The mourners might, if they wished, adjourn to waiting-rooms, where open fires kept them comfortable if not comforted. In due course they transferred to a funeral train which took them to the vast Rookwood cemetery near Lidcombe. Later the trains also travelled to Woronora Cemetery at Sutherland. At Rookwood the cortège was received at another mortuary station, also designed by James Barnet, ornate and solemn, fully in keeping with the Regent Street structure, but with a lofty gothic arch through which steam trains could proceed. For seventy years this station served the dead. As motor funerals became the rule, it fell into disuse. After twenty years of desolation, the lovely little building was purchased for $200 by a Canberra church. It was dismantled and hauled, sculptured angels and all, all the way to Canberra. Re-erected in Ainslie, it is now All Saints', one of the prettiest little churches in Australia.

However, the Regent Street Mortuary Station will remain *in situ*. After its many decades in part-time use as a parcels depot, preyed upon by vandals and souvenir-hunters, the State Rail Authority included it in a large-scale restoration plan. The Mortuary Station will live again as an exhibition terminal for historic or special trains, as well as being a permanent centre for railway displays.

Entrance Gate
Victoria Barracks
Paddington

Paddington

Until 1870 Sydney was a garrison town. For their time the George Street Barracks were the largest in the Empire, the fortress walls enclosing more than six hectares of priceless city property. It was, therefore, a commercial decision to build new military barracks in 'the most wild looking place . . . barren sandhills with patches of scrub, hills and hollows galore with much lowlying flat and swamp'.

This was today's pretty trendy Paddington.

Victoria Barracks, which, in spite of its name, is Regency-style, was designed by capable George Barney who also built Fort Denison (Pinchgut) and reconstructed Circular Quay. The work took seven years, 1841–48, and was carried out by convict gangs under the supervision of free masons and carpenters. The first regiment to occupy the new barracks was the 11th (North Devonshire) Regiment of Foot, many of whose senior officers had fought at Waterloo. Victoria Barracks is now the permanent headquarters of the Eastern Command (NSW).

The natural megalomania of the Victorians ran wild when they were given unlimited space and plentiful forced labour. From the grassy expanse of the parade ground the 225-metre length of the main building is awesome. In this structure the private soldiers lived with their families, in cramped quarters where, as one of them recorded, 'you cannot turn about without skinning your arse'. Though their life was peaceful and uneventful they had a lean time on their miserable pay. Wives wove cabbage-tree hats and sold them outside the Barracks wall, and the soldiers' children hawked mutton pies,

The 'Rectory' PADDINGTON

pickled oysters, and 'pottles of aperient native plums' to people watering their horses at the standpipe near the Barracks. This old watering-place is still marked by a pump.

The Barracks dominated Paddington from the beginning. A mushroom village of mean shacks – 'weatherboard, waterless, no lights, no sewerage and no space' – sprang up to accommodate the floods of working-class immigrants. The gentry were also beginning to establish themselves in splendid mansions, numbers of which still stand today.

Land developers moved into Paddington in the 1880s and 1890s, and the thousands of narrow-fronted terrace houses so

familiar to us today were built. They were regarded as jerry-built, meagre, of unbridled vulgarity, decked out in atrocious ironwork.

In the nineteenth century Paddington slowly declined, and by 1917 was effectively a slum. It fell upon grimy, cockroachy, even criminal times. From these it was rescued by comparatively recent updating by the intellectual, the artistic and the fashionable, who have restored the dilapidated terraces with good taste, courage and ruinous amounts of money. Today Paddington is a showplace of folk architecture, mad-hatter shops, good galleries and some exciting eating-places.

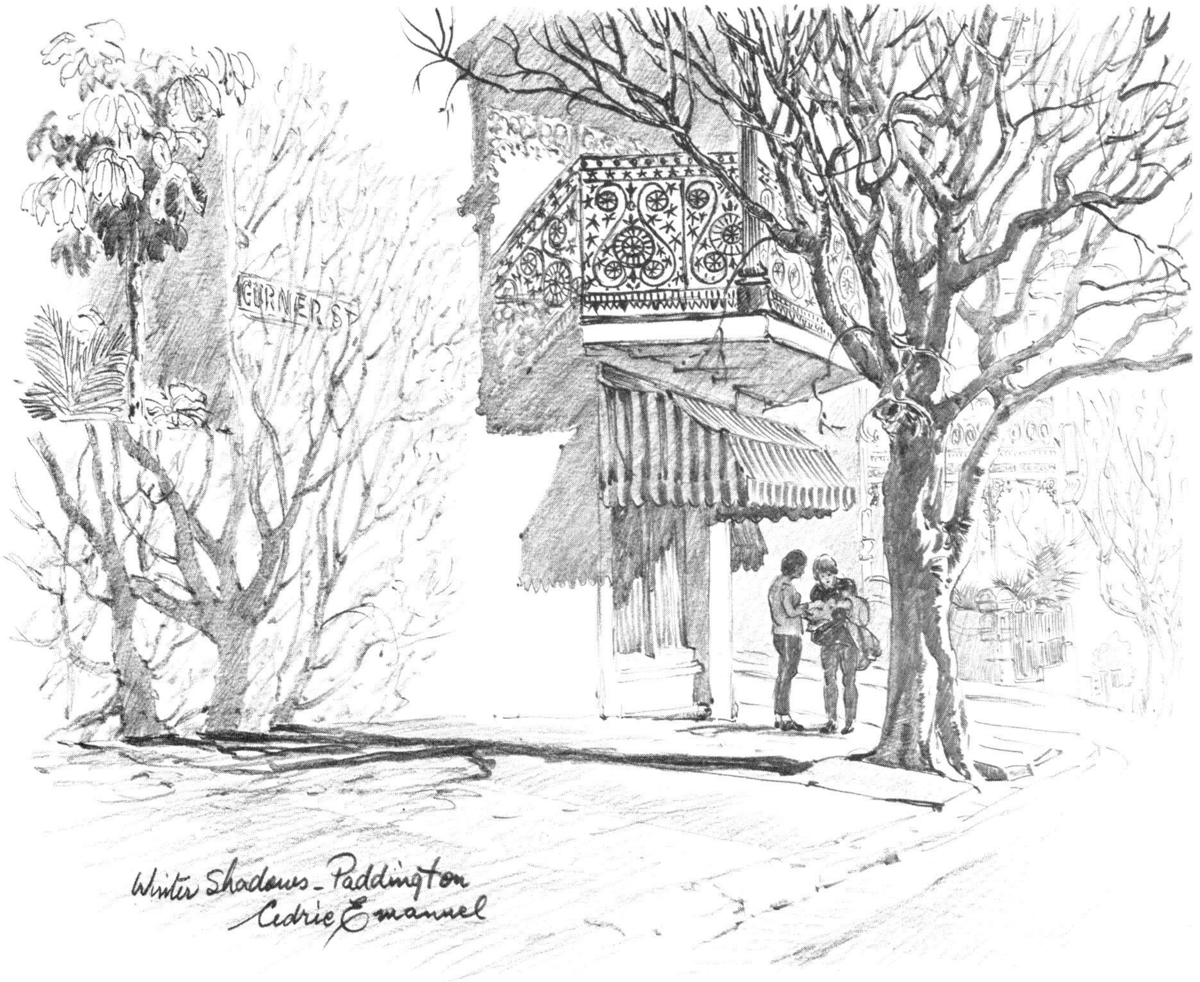

Winter Shadows – Paddington
Cedric Emanuel

Paddington
Glenmore Road

Cedric Emanuel

The El Alamein Fountain.
Kings Cross, Sydney.

King's Cross

King's Cross is a weird, electric place by night, exorbitant, often as bent as a bicycle wheel, offering venal and vulgar pleasures as well as four-cornered ones. It swims out of the dusk like a blob of spilled oil, all rainbows and reflections, and gamesome groups of middle-aged tourists, noosed with cameras and excitedly speculating whether the epicene youth in an exoskeleton of painted leather is a drug pusher.

Upon these aliens, the austerely-clad old voluptuary spidering in the coffee bar smiles his abstracted scholar's smile; the adolescent prostitute heaves up her Luxaflex eyelashes and looks right through them. The boy sitting on his kidneys beside the El Alamein Fountain, soaked with the spray, does not even glance their way as they boldly shoot off their flashes and take his picture for a souvenir.

King's Cross in the daytime is something entirely different. One sees how minikin the place is, taking up about a centimetre on the map. The charm of Darlinghurst Road, heart of the Cross, is that it is always sunny; it has a fortunate north-eastern lie. There's a great smell of roasting coffee, the patisseries are full of fresh cakes, tiny shop windows gape with the moist maculated mouths of orchids. A Hare Krishna monk floats past, suspended in a dozen yards of apricot cotton, shaven head rimmed in metal down.

In the daytime, one sees that King's Cross is truly a village, one of the several sewn indistinguishably edge to edge in the municipal ward of Fitzroy. This particular village, already well-established when the intersection of five streets was officially named Queen's Cross in 1897, picked up its present name when the Cross was renamed to honour King Edward VII in 1905. It has passed through all kinds of phases, often raffish, and has been no stranger to gang warfare, razor-slashing, illegal gambling, sly grogging, and street prostitution. At present it is at its lowest level for a century, the centre

Kings Cross 1981
Cedric Emanuel

77

Elizabeth Bay House

of the strip and massage industry, hardcore porno, and every form of dubious entertainment.

Yet King's Cross has many beautiful things. The El Alamein fountain is a dream, bluish, shot with light, sparrows and bulbuls flickering around in the spray. The El Alamein, which commemorates the desert battle, was installed in 1961. Most Sydneysiders call it 'the dandelion fountain'.

Just around the corner from the Cross, in Onslow Avenue, is a survivor of the magnificent mansions that were built below Darlinghurst Ridge in the middle years of last century. This is Elizabeth Bay House, built by John Verge for Alexander McLeay, Speaker of the first representative Legislative Council. McLeay was haughty and imperious; like John Macarthur he modelled himself on the republican Romans. He was an ardent botanist and collector.

The house, a perfect beauty, fell upon hard times. It became a boarding house, flats, goodness knows what. In 1963 the State Planning Authority snatched it from the hands of cruel developers, and it has been gloriously restored. It is completely in period. In the drawing rooms even curtains and carpets were specially woven to the original designs.

The marvellous staircase, which wafts up from the hall under a 'lantern' roof 15 metres high, is alone worth the price of admission, which is modest enough.

The pretty terraces, the iron lace balconies begin at King's Cross, and come into full bloom in Paddington, which is not so far away.

Centennial Park

We owe Centennial Park to the jolly Dick Whittington of Victorian Sydney, Charles Moore, thrice Mayor. It was he who cast a greedy civic eye on the Sydney Common. Here settlers grazed cows and goats, gentlemen ventured in swan-shooting parties, and paupers and runaways set up hidden wurlies amongst the reeds and scrub.

The Victoria Barracks was built on the north side of the Common and some of the land was sold off to form, one conjectures, the suburbs of Kensington, Randwick and part of Zetland. Most did not know, and the rest had forgotten, that the Common had been legally granted to the people of Sydney. Fortunately Charles Moore, rummaging through old documents, discovered the grant.

After long wrangling and some litigation the Government conceded the title as far as the unsold land was concerned, and the Common became 'a great national property', a complex of parks, semi-wilderness, lakes, golf links.

Centennial Park was opened on the first hundred-year anniversary of the founding of the colony, that is, 26 January 1888. It was a bright clear day, and on the 'hills and flats of the erstwhile Lachlan Swamps was . . . an assemblage almost as multifarious as the multitude of Hannibal'.

Since then Centennial Park, together with its flock of surrounding amenities, including the golf links, the Show Ground and Randwick Racecourse, has been the city's most important wide-open space.

Aside from an abortive official attempt in the early 1970s to convert the area into a new and rather grand sports complex, Centennial Park has remained, not as Mayor Charles Moore found it – 'with no residences, fencings or improvements, but plenty of geebungs, five-corners, and native currants', but as he directed it should be, 'a countryside in the midst of a city'. It is only fair to add that the Premier of the time, Sir Henry Parkes, was also very strong for Centennial Park. He thought it should contain a noble pantheon where the city's great could be enshrined after death. Fortunately this did not come about.

Centennial Park is a great place for dogs and children, a jumping, running wild, tree-climbing place, with mud to slosh in and swamps that squelch. The park covers over 200 hectares but seems even larger; they say there are 8 kilometres of iron picket fence, but the terrain is so irregular that mostly you don't guess a fence is there. In someone's good phrase, there's a variety of countryside here.

Rose Bay

Rose Bay is the largest bay on Sydney Harbour, a deep sparkling half-moon with Point Piper doing its best to enclose it on the west, and the Vaucluse peninsula swooping away on the east. Rose Bay has escaped being trendy; it is a comfortable maritime suburb whose every short bay street presents a picture of big trees, placid sea, and the brilliant cityscape beyond.

The Aboriginals called the bay Pannerong, meaning 'blood'. It was the sacred site for ritual battle. The first white men to live there were convict workers at the salt boilers, set up on the beach in 1805. Later the wealthy saw what a beautiful place it was, and consequently Rose Bay still has many handsome mansions to show. Some of these are now exclusive schools – Cranbrook, built by Robert Tooth the brewer in 1859; Kambala, its nucleus a house belonging to Captain Dumaresq, of Governor Darling's family but much of the present structure designed by the architect Horbury Hunt. This marvellously funny fellow also created the formidable Sacred Heart Convent, which mounts majestically a hill above Rose Bay. It too incorporates an original house, Claremont, built in 1852.

Horbury Hunt, a tiny eccentric Canadian, arrived in Sydney in 1862. He rode a bicycle, which he had converted into an architectural office, complete with attached drawing board. He kept sheets of paper in his hat. His work is usually fresh, simple and original, and the Sacred Heart convent and school seem rather ponderous for him. Like a castle it looks down over its gardens at the sunlit bay, but it's a mellow castle, with a centenary in 1984.

Vaucluse

Vaucluse is of rocky, irregular terrain, and herein lies so much of its idiosyncratic charm. Walkways descend between ferny clifflets, flights of steps show us gemmy glimpses of seascape one moment and pink bosses of pigface in some secluded rock garden the next.

Vaucluse takes its name from the property owned by Sir Henry Browne Hayes, the unlikely convict, who abducted an unwilling and spirited Corkonian heiress in 1797. In spite of his being but little pockmarked and having remarkable whiskers the lady did not take to him. She was restored to her Papa, and Sir Henry was transported. He was a born trouble-

maker and, though a life-sentence convict, behaved to all in New South Wales as though he were visiting royalty.

He bought the lovely estate of Vaucluse in 1803, and it is thought his small stone house is incorporated into the present structure. Being afraid of snakes, Sir Henry imported 152 tonnes of Irish soil. It arrived in biscuit barrels and was dug into a two-metre trench which ran around the house. The Irish superintendent of convicts and the many Irish prisoners in the gang of seventy-five wept over the chocolate soil and begged Sir Henry for handfuls of it. 'Take it and welcome,' he said.

Sir Henry's later career was one of constant misadventure. He returned to Ireland in 1812, and died in his native Cork in the odour of sanctity. Born into a lowlier class he would undoubtedly have ended on the scaffold.

William Charles Wentworth bought the Vaucluse estate in 1827. Wentworth, editor, explorer, elder statesman, was born on a vessel of the disastrous Second Fleet, en route to Australia. His mother, Catherine Crowley, was transported for thieving clothing. His father, D'Arcy Wentworth, left England just ahead of an arrest for highway robbery. D'Arcy Wentworth became a well-known surgeon and landowner, and died a wealthy and respected man. He sent William, at the age of eight, off to England for a good education, and for this we are indebted to him.

As a rich young radical, W.C. Wentworth was passionately involved in everything he undertook. In 1813 at the age of twenty-two he, with Blaxland and Lawson, found a way over the colony's Great Wall of China, the Blue Mountains, which barred all enterprise to the west.

Wentworth inaugurated the protests which led to the introduction of many civil liberties such as free speech, the right to hold public meetings, and trial by jury. Still his major and lifelong interest was the creation of a constitutional and representative government in a colony hitherto ruled arbitrarily by a Governor responsible only to the British Government, which was grossly ignorant of the needs and desires of its distant colony.

At Vaucluse Wentworth built 'a genteel dwelling house' which has seen little change in a century and a half. It is an endearing mingling of Gothic and old colonial.

In spite of the many charms of the Henry VIII-type kitchen, the drawing room is my favourite. Instead of wallpaper, painted panels adorn the walls. These were done by a convict, Bryant Payne, who ran away several times in the process. These panels feature formal entwinements of roses, convolvulus and passionflowers, probably painted from specimens from Wentworth's garden.

The house is full of intriguing oddments, period garments, pictures of that long-gone Sydney, portraits, china, Venetian glass, alabaster. Much of this has been bequeathed to the Trust by collectors. The chandeliers are especially worth noting.

William Charles Wentworth died in England in 1872. His body was returned to Sydney, given a state funeral and interred in the family vault, which is just a little stroll away in Chapel Road.

In the Rose Garden

Parsley Bay

Next door to Vaucluse Bay is the sheltered blue cranny of Parsley Bay. Long ago this perfect picnic place was one of those reedy brackish marshes so characteristic of the shores of Sydney Harbour. It seems to have been drying out by the time Phillip's exploratory boat nosed in, 22 January 1788. They landed and picked a curly-leaved greenstuff that reminded them of parsley, hence the present name. There is now a charming park with tall trees all around, an enclosed swimming pool, and the quaintest bridge by which you may cross from one side of Parsley Bay to the other.

Watson's Bay

The suburb of Watson's Bay runs down to a flat, picturesque little foreshore, trig and well kept. It has an archaic look as though it were still a fishing village. The streets are little more than lanes, and there are some nice old stone cottages. The blue sky, the coral trees, the jetty where housewives are buying fish from a boatman and where someone is weighing a shark on the big–game hoist, all add to the relaxed atmosphere of this countrified, serene suburb.

To Watson's Bay come hundreds to view the start of the internationally-contested Sydney to Hobart race, one of the world's great long-distance sailing races.

There are numbers of things to look at in Watson's Bay: the Moreton Bay fig tree on the waterfront under which Governor Macquarie and his party picnicked in 1811; the obelisk which marks the completion of the eight-mile Old South Head Road by the soldiers of the 73rd 'reghtment'. This

Watson's Bay
SYDNEY HARBOUR.

92

followed the old track marked out by the signal station crew. St Peter's Church is a simple little village church by Edmund Blacket. It was built in 1864, 'to be the first building to greet the eyes of newcomers to Sydney'. It has a funny little gallery, and its organ used to be owned by the Emperor Napoleon. Dunbar House, in Robertson Park, is a comely old colonial. Built before 1840 for the Colonial Treasurer, it is named for the tragic immigrant ship which smashed into the Gap cliffs on a wintry night in 1857, there being only one survivor.

Camp Cove

Camp Cove is a lovely little crescent tucked down behind the giant's breakwater of South Head. Close to the end of Pacific Street is the Victorian house of that interesting Russian explorer-biologist, Nicolaus Miklouho-Maclay. Here in the late 1880s he established the first biological research station in Australia. From the footpath on the northern side you may spot his monogram engraved on one of the house's pillars.

On the shore is the obelisk which records Captain Phillip's landing here on 21 January 1788, when he sailed up from his unsatisfactory Botany Bay camp to explore unknown Port Jackson. So this is, as far as we know, white men's first landing place within Sydney Harbour.

Worth seeing is the tiny, atticked doll's house in Cove Street, perfectly restored, and reputed to be the first cottage built in Camp Cove.

This little Cove has always been associated with the pilots, who used to row out in open boats. Next door Watson's Bay was the inspection point for ships' documents, and customs and medical examination. There are several navigational marks still remaining from those days of sail.

About 800 metres offshore, the ebbing tide creams over the rocky shoal called the Sow and Pigs. This divides the fairway to the main harbour into two channels. Always a menace to shipping, the Sow and Pigs were marked by lightships for many years; the most noticeable of their present warning complex is the tall striped tripod. The rocks are a natural rounding point for yacht races, and in fact are mentioned in the description of the first recorded race in Sydney Harbour, when the boats' crews of two British warships competed for a purse of Spanish dollars.

The Hornby Light

Manly

Manly residents have always called their town The Village. It is a real child of the salt and sand. The Municipality comprises over 27 kilometres of the most superb surf coastline in the world. And that's only on one side. On the other is the Harbour.

In the early 1980s The Village refurbished its wharves, shopping centre and shoreline, and it is now one of the most charming of holiday places. Millions of visitors annually find it so, though it is only eleven kilometres by ferry from Circular Quay.

Manly made the Sydney map before Sydney itself. When Captain Phillip realised that his new settlers couldn't continue floundering around in the Botany Bay swamps, he and some of his young men sailed up the coast to Port Jackson. On a summer day full of cicadas and apple-gum bloom, the little boat dawdled along in the shade of towering North Head, and its occupants had a peaceful encounter with a band of local residents.

'Manly coves!' Phillip is reported to have observed.

A landing was made in one of the delicious bays, the date was 21 January 1788. There followed the first night ever spent in Port Jackson, in the lee of Smedley's Point. As this was the first vice-regal visit, The Village was the original seat (though dampish and uncomfortable) of British Government in Sydney.

Harbour Waterfront MANLY

The Spit Bridge

The Spit Bridge is the bottleneck met by the Manly and north-bound traffic that swirls down the precipitous Spit Hill from the Junction. The unwinding view is a wonderful one, especially at sunset, when the Spit's myriad little boats are painted pink, and the polished water of Pearl Bay reflects dazzling windows from Beauty Point to Seaforth Bluff. For many years vehicles, teams and all were ferried over the narrow channel on punts. Ponderous in weight and strength were those ox waggons, built like ships to withstand all the forces of nature and of time. They brought to Sydney timber, produce, fodder and lime from the shellbanks of Pittwater.

At a later date the punts carried motor vehicles and pedestrians and, after the tram service to Manly started about 1913, a specially-fitted punt occasionally ferried across a tram, not as a part of the passenger service, but to augment the existing Manly-Narrabeen tram fleet during surf carnivals and important football matches.

The present bridge replaces a wooden one which stood until 1958. Its centre rises drawbridge style to let boats pass under into the hundred bays and inlets of Middle Harbour which stretch beyond.

Hunter's Hill

For nearly half a century no one wanted what we know today as Hunter's Hill. The place had poor soil, was tick-infested, and benighted wallaby and koala hunters were worried by fairy voices wailing about their camps in the dark. Undoubtedly these fairies were of the same race as those others that unnerved lonely sentries during Sydney's first months. 'Warra warra,' they whispered, and it was not until much time had gone by that it was understood that these words meant 'Go away!'

Serious settlement upon the many-bayed, narrow peninsula which separates the Parramatta and Lane Cove Rivers did not begin until 1834. That year the remarkable business woman, Mary Reiby the emancipist, built a riverside cottage near present-day Fig Tree Bridge. Didier Joubert bought the cottage in 1847, and from this point on the river he and his son Numa operated a fleet of Lane Cove ferries for forty-six years. The Joubert home and Mary Reiby's as well were demolished in 1961.

Hunter's Hill's early nickname, 'the French village', is due solely to Joubert Frères, whom we imagine as a jolly pair of Cheerybles from Bordeaux, intent on dabbing the colonial

Gladesville Bridge,
Parramatta River

PARRAMATTA RIVER
nd Gladesville Bridge from Hunters Hill   Adrie Emanuel

Cedric Emanuel The Crescent Hunter's Hill

woodlands wild with a little chic. But Jules Joubert, his brother Didier and their partner the Comte de Milhau were accomplished and comfortably wealthy men. They were the first large-scale speculative builders in Sydney. The Jouberts began to build about 1848 and it is said that two hundred of their houses are still standing in Hunter's Hill. The partners used indigenous materials wherever possible, but they imported French and Italian masons, as well as shiploads of European tiles, glass, marble and decorative fittings.

Hunter's Hill, therefore, though not historic in the usual sense, is a curious and delightful place to explore. The houses are not all grand by any means. Many are the handsomest bijou cottages, some built at a later date in the Joubert manner by Lombard stoneworkers who put up at the Garibaldi Inn. The 1861 inn is on the corner of Ferry and Alexander Streets.

Hunter's Hill has a loved look, and this is very evident in the houses, whether they are mousy cottages of soft grey stone, or the fanciful Victorian beauties, Wybalena, Waiwera and St Ives. Two other great houses, though built in the Victorian era, are severe and classical, Passy with its twin stairs curving like fern fronds, and Merimbah, built by the Comte de Milhau and for all the world like a transplanted chateau.

103

From the end of the nineteenth century Clarke's Point, which projects into the Parramatta River on the south-east, was occupied by Woolwich Dock, a noted shipyard, built to accommodate ships over 23,000 tonnes. The last ship, a harbour ferry, was launched in 1954. The State Government eventually resumed the land and placed it in the care of Hunter's Hill Council. The lovely point is now a handsome reserve, looking towards the Sydney skyline over the islands and peninsulas and busy harbour waters. The park is fittingly named for John Clarke, the first settler in Woolwich.

Alexander Street at Ferry St.

Cedric Emanuel

Nos 1+3 Foss St

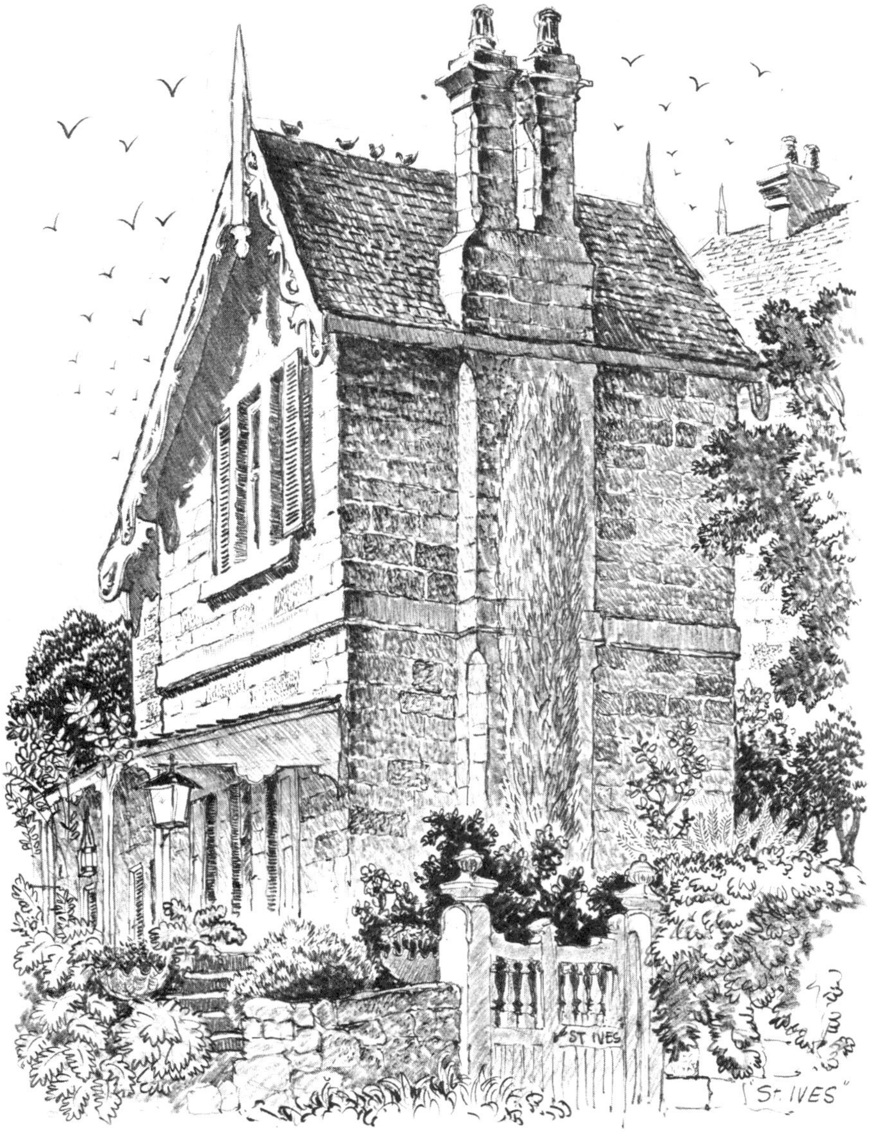
ST IVES
"St. IVES"

"Innisfree" Hunters Hill

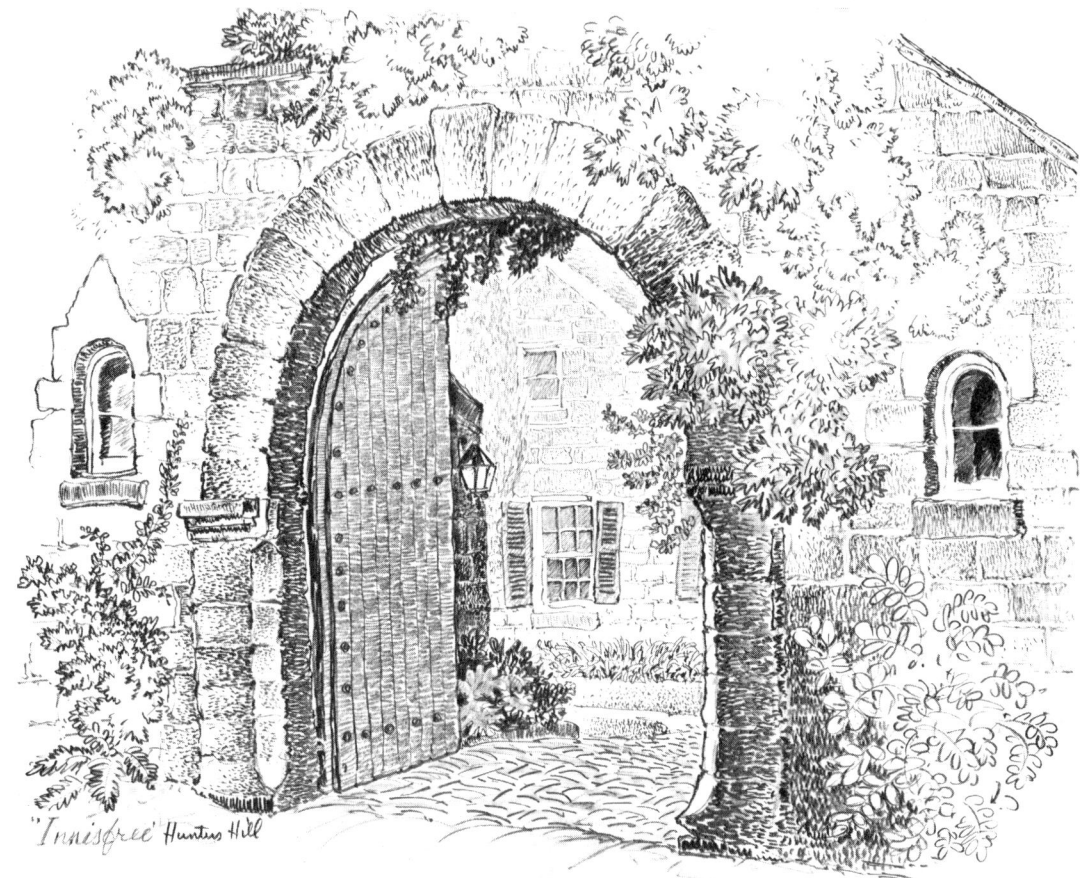

The Glebe

For collectors of quaint Sydney architecture, from High Victorian confectionery to decrepit tiny cottages of hen-pecked stone, the Glebe is the place. The elderly suburb has the most fortunate lie; its streets are always full of sunshine, the trees are thicker and greener there. The whole place is like a contented old cat snoozing its days away. Yet there's a sense of the sea, even though maritime industry is fast moving away from Darling Harbour and Blackwattle Bay.

The Glebe became that when Governor Phillip, in 1789, granted 162 hectares to the Established Church in the person of the shy, sickly curate, the Reverend Richard Johnson. No church, just a glebe. The district was called the Kangaroo Ground, and we are told it looked like Sherwood Forest and was populated by ticks and bright parrots. A huge salt swamp lay at the foot of the gentle hills running down to Blackwattle Bay. Here the rushcutters worked, gathering thatch for the first houses of Sydney. This swamp, now Wentworth Park sportsgrounds, became from the mid-1800s a nauseatingly befouled place. It took the drainage from the abattoirs, the sugar refinery and the brewery and was also a sewerage out-fall. Industry had come to the Glebe as well as small farmers, the odd adventurous gentleman who built a grand house in sylvan seclusion, orchardists and boatbuilders.

The building of Sydney University and several large hospitals close to the Parramatta Road contributed to the growth of the Glebe as a dormitory area for students and nursing staffs. The architecture therefore is amazingly varied, ranging from senile cottages with sagging shutters and reeling gates to the impressive Edwardian terraces in Pyrmont Bridge Road. There are a few old homes dating from the first occupation of the Glebe forest, some woefully neglected, barely keeping afloat in a sea of unpruned greenery. Others have always been occupied. Toxteth House, in Avenue Road, for instance, was built between 1828 and 1831. It is now portion of St Scholastica's Convent for girls.

But most of the Glebe is Victorian. The visitor wanders amongst ornate brickwork, often set in herringbone patterns above doors or in porches, etched glass doors, plaster festoons and rosettes, ravishing chimneypots. Queen of Victorian Glebe is the Town Hall, banana-coloured, foursquare, a lobster-leg spike on every possible corner. It was erected in 1880.

Arcadia Road, Glebe

Parramatta

Governor Phillip established Parramatta nine months after Sydney. By 1794 it found itself at the end of 'a quite good road' which began at Sydney Cove and marched out through the trackless forests that surrounded the midget settlement. In summer the highway was swept with blinding clouds of dust, in winter it had potholes that drowned bullocks. All the year round it was beset by bushrangers and runaway convicts. This quite good road is still called the Parramatta Road.

Cedric Emanuel

Old Government House
Parramatta.

George Bell's Horse Trough

The Anderson Fountain 1882

From the beginning Parramatta was a prosperous, fascinating town. The governors loved it. It was a restful place after the squabbles and badmouthing of Sydney. By 1791 there was a large, elegant Government House standing above a graceful loop of river, wide maize paddocks, many stone prisoners' huts, a considerable military establishment, and some fine gentlemen's farms.

Old Government House is the oldest public building in Australia. White, with green shutters and an austere lack of ornament, it has the daintiness which comes from perfect proportions.

Just inside the gothic gates is an obelisk marking the place where, in 1847, Governor Fitzroy's carriage overturned and his wife and aide de camp were 'dashed to pieces against a mighty oak'. Lady Mary, daughter of the Duke of Richmond, was extremely popular, and Sydney would have preferred the demise of her husband, interestingly described as 'a vulgar voluptuary and systematic Sybarite . . . a mindless puppet . . . in no sense a gentleman'. Nevertheless when he retired the colonists, perhaps in relief, gave him a purse of two thousand guineas.

His son George was a keen hunter and established a pack, well turned out in pink, to hunt the dingo. The farmers, whose paddocks were trampled, fences broken and citrus hedges knocked down, were advertised as being 'highly delighted at this realisation in Australia of the good old field sports of the Mother Country'.

The Fitzroy family lived in the present front building, as did Governor Macquarie. The entire structure is full of shades . . . Governor Bligh bellowing, addressing soldiers and aides alike as 'bastards and wretches', his daughter, Mary Putland, an affected and testy little woman, occasionally flinging a plate or candlestick at her parent's head.

After the governors left Old Government House, the building stood empty for a long time. Then it became a fashionable boarding house. One of its upstairs rooms was often used as a surgery. In 1878 Dr Walter Brown of Brislington performed one of the first successful ovariotomies. For more than fifty years from 1910 it was the King's School Junior Boarding House. It then passed into the hands of the National Trust, and by 1970 was sufficiently restored for Queen Elizabeth II to declare it open to the public. It is but one of the many historic buildings, military and civil, that adorn Parramatta.

The finest house open for inspection is Surgeon Harris's

GEORGE ST— PARRAMATTA – Tudor Gatehouse   Cedric Emanuel

Experiment Farm Cottage, magnificently restored by the Trust, and refurnished in the period 1798-1840. Historic as it is, the land upon which it stands is more so, for it is here that the Cornish convict James Ruse 'sowed the forst grain'. Ruse, a silent man and model prisoner, had been a husbandman. He asked permission of the Governor to settle on the land and become, if possible, self-supporting. Phillip had a little land cleared for him. It was he who christened the plot Experiment Farm. He gave Ruse what tools he could and a few bushels of grain from the Government's first scant harvest in 1789. Thus we note that Ruse did not sow the first grain as he claims on his tombstone. He was the first private settler who success-fully sowed grain. He had no animal fertiliser, only com-posted straw. He had no plough; the earth was broken with the hoe. His only farm labourer was his wife Elizabeth, the first woman convict emancipated in the colony. Some of his tools can now be seen at Experiment Farm.

Ruse defeated caterpillars, thieving convicts, and drought, and, gathering in a poverty-stricken harvest, he made the proud gesture of relinquishing his claim to government rations. Phillip showed his appreciation by granting Ruse a further thirteen hectares, and building him a brick house. After Ruse went off to farm on the Hawkesbury and other places, Surgeon John Harris bought the farm, and built a handsome new house. Harris was a conceited, extraordinarily good-looking man, and is credited with being the first doctor to take a supply of fresh cowpock to Parramatta.

His house, built in 1798, is an endearing place, with a

War Memorial

particularly beautiful Georgian doorway with oval fanlight. The courtyard has a wonderful look of old Parramatta, sunny and sheltered, paved with freckled convict bricks of golden colour. Shady trees, a straw bee skep, a well with a pump and a cottage garden of pinks, lamb's ear and tumbling violas bring thoughts of yesteryear. Surely John and Elizabeth Macarthur must have sometimes sat here with their gentlemanly neighbour?

Parramatta was the home of many notable people, but somehow the most memorable was the eighteenth-century

Experiment Farm Cottage

lady Elizabeth Macarthur. For almost half a century she lived at Elizabeth Farm, which is still standing, reared a famous family, managed the property, and wrote vivacious letters. The shy daughter of a country gentleman, she married in 1788 the 21-year-old John Macarthur. This extraordinary man was brave, quarrelsome and of highly nervous temperament. In a century notable for gross incivilities, his annihilating remarks stand alone. To have dealings with the father of the Australian wool industry was to feature in his letters, sooner or later as a Wretch, a Reptile, a Bloodsucker, Tyrant or Cockatrice.

Macarthur's resolute pursuit of the English market for Australian grown wool was as important a factor in the establishment of the industry as was his intelligent breeding for finer staple and heavier yield.

Elizabeth's life with this fiery particle was not easy, though he was a courtly husband and a father beloved by his children. As time went on he suffered from 'Dreadful Glooms' interspersed by bouts of manic energy. Becoming quite deranged, he was confined to the library of Elizabeth Farm. He believed himself poisoned, that his loyal sons had deserted him, that Elizabeth was unfaithful. He was removed to his large pastoral grant of Camden Park and spent his last years mostly in childlike cheerfulness.

John died in 1834, still alienated from his devoted wife. A teardrop stains the brittle page on which she wrote: 'The fountain of my eyes which I believed to be dry opened anew.' Sixteen years later she was laid to rest beside her husband at Camden Park.

The trees the Macarthurs planted still surround Elizabeth Farm. Through them shine the lights of Parramatta City, an exploding, forward-looking metropolis which probably still considers Sydney 'the river mouth', as it did in 1800.

Linden House

The Hawkesbury

One place to which we return again and again is the Hawkesbury, the Sydneysider's familiar name for both river and rural district, approximately 55 kilometres west and north-west of the humming city. The Hawkesbury river complex is enormous, draining more than 20,000 square kilometres. The main stream is 480 kilometres long. It is navigable for 95 kilometres by deep-draught boats, and 135 kilometres for little craft. The Hawkesbury forms the north and western boundaries of Sydney.

It is a land of flat silvery landscapes, wind-ruffled crops,

Governor Lachlan Macquarie

RICHMOND 4
KURRAJONG 11
LITHGOW 53
BLACKTOWN
CAMDEN 38
108 SINGLETON SYDNEY 35
57 PUTTY PARRAMATTA 20
3½ WILBERFORCE
9 SACKVILLE
16 COLO RIVER

Miles from
WINDSOR
(before conversion)
to Km

ruined windmills and brindled inland skies. The Blue Mountains shoulder away the westerlies, and flood its many creeks with their huge run-off. It's a land of horse studs, somnolent villages and colonial houses built without any architectural hyperbole at all.

The blacks called the river Deerubbin, of which the meaning has been lost. And in a sense the land of Deerubbin is lost too; the Victorian age did not touch it, and it holds on to itself and its timelessness as though in a conspiracy against modernism.

This area was the campagna. It fed Sydney but was different from Sydney. This is still so. Along this ambling, jungle-green river are serene little towns, named by Governor Macquarie and much influenced by the timeless good taste of his architect Greenway.

Windsor is the first, rich with quaint or historic buildings, its graveyard full of familiar names. The Court House, now agreeably denuded of all its Victorian accretions, is a Greenway design (circa 1822). It has exceptional cedar joinery, and a unique portrait of Macquarie. Down the hill from the Court House is an adorable family of sandstock and stone cottages restored by the National Trust.

St Matthew's in Moses Street is to my mind Greenway's

117

most distinctive building, and the most superbly sited. However, there are some odd references to this church throughout
the century and a half since it was consecrated by Samuel
Marsden, principal chaplain of the colony; 'strange' is a word
often used of it.

To those waggoners and foot travellers creeping across the
country from the foothills of the Blue Mountains, it must
have seemed like a signal station: 'Beyond here is the civilised
world', was its message. Indeed this thought may have been
in Greenway's mind, for the octagonal cupola which crowns

St Matthew's Church

St Matthew's Church

the tower is uncannily reminiscent of the earlier lighthouse on Sydney's South Head.

The church is built of exceptionally handsome convict bricks, which the sunshine turns to the colour of new banksia cobs. Its original shingle roof, restored many times, was replaced with copper in 1958, and its foundation stone, laid by Macquarie, is on the outer wall of the porch. Inside this porch you will find an aged Bible. This, together with the church bell and the clock in the tower, was presented to the congregation by George IV. (See the last page of the colour section.)

Richmond Farm

St Matthew's building was marked by the usual colonial hazards. When Governor Macquarie put down the foundation stone in October 1817, he placed a holey dollar beneath it. This Spanish dollar was part of the peculiar currency of the period and worth about a third of a guinea. That very night the dollar was whipped away by some hard case. Macquarie laid the stone again, and put down another dollar which also went missing. Presumably after this the irate Scotsman put down only the stone, as it was not disturbed again.

The churchyard was here before the church. Andrew Thompson lies here, that noted convict after whom Thompson Square was named. 'Good and worthy', Governor Macquarie, who attended his funeral, said of him. He died from a lung complaint brought on by his heroic labours in the great flood of 1807, when he worked without sleeping for sixty hours in a countryside flooded by a 16-metre rise.

Andrew Thompson is reported to have saved many lives. Of course, he had his enemies. The military enclave, which was so affronted by the Governor's liberal attitude towards emancipists, had its spokesman in the fiery John Macarthur. 'his death . . . is an earnest of the interposition of Providence to save the colony from Utter Ruin. Never was there a more artful or a greater knave.'

Thompson's house still stands, a modest Georgian farmhouse, on his original grant of Agnes Bank, which is south of Richmond near the Castlereagh Road.

Just down the road from St Matthew's is the Old Rectory, a Georgian country house as symmetrical as a clock. It was erected by William Cox who built the Court House. He also

Rose Cottage, Wilberforce

Peninsula House, Windsor

St Matthew's Rectory

was responsible for putting the first road across the Blue Mountains. The interior of the house is ornamented with cedar joinery and Italianate folding interior window shutters. It must have been a delightful home. Here Sam Marsden died in 1858, not in a fit of apoplexy as one might have expected, but calmly and peacefully whilst visiting his friend, Mr Styles, the Windsor parson.

The river here is most natural, with irregular sandy beaches and spits, many casuarinas and willows and swimmers and family picnics on the sand.

In Livingstone Street stands the Peninsular House, where the astronomer John Tebbutt lived and observed all kinds of astronomical phenomena. (There are two Tebbutt's Comets.) Born in 1834, and educated in Windsor, the shy, brilliant John Tebbutt devoted most of his life to astronomy, winning international recognition. The Peninsular House is a characteristic old colonial, with slate roof, small-paned windows with stone sills, a shady, flagged verandah. The observatory is the more unusual structure with its somewhat ecclesiastical porch, its dome, and corners tick-tack-toed with white stone.

Windsor was really a military settlement for a long time. The soldiers were often called upon to help in times of harvesting, and indeed many of them, when their time expired, took up land around the river. There are still numbers of families that bear the names of troopers, especially from Macquarie's 73rd Regiment.

Nearly all Windsor's folktales, though, relate to the terrible floods which have ravaged it time and time again. They are completely unpredictable, although nowadays their excesses are checked by the Warragamba Dam. The floods have been a feature of the Hawkesbury's ancient life; when the engineers began to put down the caissons for a bridge at Peat's Ferry Road, they did not strike hard rock until they had penetrated 73.5 metres of alluvial silt.

In 1864 an eyewitness reported: 'The Toll Bar house and the Windsor Hotel were completely carried away. The counter floated out of Holden's with tumblers and jugs standing on it, just as it had been before the occupants hurriedly left. I saw furniture drifting along the river. There was a cow on a barley

Tebbutt Observatory

SACRED
to
The Mem of
CHRISTOPHER
...

SACRED
To The
MEMORY of
RICHARD HAYES
Who Departed This Life
January 11 1812
Aged 50 Years

SACRED
to
the MEMORY of
WILLM HAYES
Who Departed the,
...

W.H

HERE LIES THE BODY
of ROBERT MCKENZIE
WHO DEPARTED THIS LIFE
FEBY 19th 1825 aged 53
Through blustery gales
and rolling WAVES
I have been tossed to x fro
Now at last by Gods desire
I have reached Harbour here
Now within Anchor love I lie
With many of my fleet
Tomorrow again I will arise to
My Saviour Christ to meet

mow, two children on a hencoop. The trees were full of snakes . . . screaming horses were caught in wire . . .'

At Ebenezer, perched above the curling river, is a little church amongst old graves and flowerbeds. With its many-paned windows and enormously thick stone walls it looks rather like a Hebridean house. It is the oldest church building in Australia. In 1802 a party of Presbyterian immigrants from the Scottish Border settled near Portland Heads. They had no minister, only an elder, James Mein, who conducted services in private houses and taught catechism in the fields. A kindly settler gave the group 1.6 hectares to be Church property. This they called Ebenezer which means 'Hitherto hath the Lord helped us'. They built the church themselves, and to it they came by horseback and rowing boat. Many of these devout people now sleep about the church, which looks as if it will stand another two centuries.

From Hawkins' Lookout above Wiseman's Ferry one admires the broad river, its majestic greenstone breast marked with broad arrows from the water skiers that skittle across it like so many mayflies. The rich river-flats look, as Chinese river-flats do, as though they have been cultivated for thousands of years. The orange trees march almost to the banks. Ahead to the north, forested cliffs hang against the sky. Unclimbable, frowning, they look down upon the kingdom of Solomon Wiseman.

Solomon Wiseman emerges from history as a tough, brusque illiterate with extraordinary business acumen. Transported for stealing timber — and his sentence commuted from death at that — he arrived in the colony in 1806. Solomon sensibly spread it around that he had been nabbed for smuggling, then regarded as a daredevil and socially acceptable occupation. He was pardoned in 1812, and his career took off like a bomb. He went into the shipping business. In 1817 he was given a grant of 81 hectares which he selected at the Hawkesbury, in this fertile area where we now stand. He had a finger in everything, shipbuilding, trading and timber-getting. He also had a government contract for provisioning the convicts who laboured on the roads. This contract alone brought in a minimum of $7,000 a year; in those taxfree days, this was very big money.

By 1820 his fortress-like house Cobham Hall was built, and you will see it at once, half hidden in the confused lines of the white-chimneyed Hawkesbury Hotel.

Renovations and additions throughout the years have not dealt well with the Sign of the Packet, which is what Wiseman

A Hawkesbury River ferry

called his house during the long period it served as an inn. The original portion has walls nearly a metre thick.

Solomon actually established his ferry in 1827, at his private expense. It was big business, for almost to the turn of last century this was the principal crossing place for large mobs of cattle from the north bound for the Sydney markets. The cattle were either swum across or transported by punt. Threepence per head was charged for cattle swum across guided by the ferryman.

The old scamp chose his situation well. Traffic towards the coalfields and the Hunter River farming district followed the convict-hewn Old Northern Road almost as soon as the road began to take shape. Before that, northbound traffic went via Windsor, but again crossed the ford at Wiseman's Ferry.

The one portrait of Wiseman in existence shows a tail-coated gentleman with a round, fuzzy white head, close side whiskers and bleached manic eyes. Perhaps this was the tail-coat in which he was buried, complete with boots and dress sword, 'a grand finale to prodigious success'. Solomon was buried in the local church of St Mary Magdalene, to the building of which he had generously contributed. This church was ruined in successive floods, and Solomon's bones went bumping off, many being collected by souvenir hunters.

Old School House, Wilberforce 1820

John Wilson's vertical sundial St John's Church WILBERFORCE

1859 J·W·

Broken Bay, Pittwater

Botany Bay

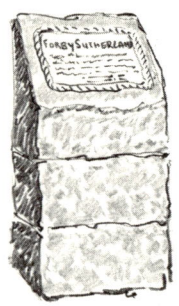

Botany Bay, in spite of the airport and the spectacular display of heavy industry, has a haunting air of the archaic. Sand oozes up between the grass roots, trees have a permanent cant before the fresh, ever-present wind. Left to itself for fifty years, Botany Bay would revert to the original water meadows that deceived Captain Cook and Joseph Banks into thinking they had observed good grassland. Cook made his first Australian landing across the bay, on Kurnell Peninsula, 28 April 1770. All the historic area has now been converted into a splendid park; bushland, tramping trails, picnic and parking areas make this a wonderful place to spend the day.

But the old worn down settlement on the north-east side of Botany Bay is still the more fascinating. The solitary stone watch tower on its green hillock was built to the order of Governor Macquarie in 1821. Here soldiers watched for foreign vessels carrying foreign flags. A customs officer watched for smugglers.

On a tiny island to the north-west of Congwong Bay is a queer little fort erected in 1885 to defend Botany Bay and the

Erected in memory of
DANIEL CARL SOLANDER
who together with Capt. JAMES COOK
and Sir JOSEPH BANKS
landed in Australia in April 1770

In grateful memory of
SIR JOSEPH BANKS
1743 - 1820
Famous British scientist who
visited these shores with
Captain JAMES COOK in 1770

BANKS

The Barrack Tower

southern approaches of Sydney. It is hard to believe that Bare Island Fort was ever taken seriously. But we must remember that in 1885 the infant colony was feeling its oats. It had just sent a contingent (readied in sixty days!) off to aid the British Army rescue doomed General Gordon, under siege at Khartoum. The little Sudan contingent, Australia's first military offering to the motherland, did not see active service, but the effect on the colony was stimulating. The Bare Island fort is evidence of this blooming national sentiment.

The fort was occupied as a permanent artillery garrison until it was taken over as a war veterans' home. The returned soldiers were, in their turn, shifted in 1963 to modern quarters at Narrabeen.

The fort and barracks, with their mysteriously curving passages and massive gun emplacements, are a curious reminder of the limitations of the military mind in the days when war belonged to sea and land and the rule book.

Phillip did right not to plant his settlement on the shores of Botany Bay. One feels that the wind blows always, Antarctic chill upon its breath. Treeless hills, combed grass, the sea's shoaly run towards the Kurnell shore – all speak of a habit of climate severer than that of Port Jackson. Phillip's greatest gift to the future generations of Sydneysiders was his own practical good sense.

Captain Cook's Memorial

Index

PRINCIPAL ROADS
DISTANCE FROM SYDNEY
To BATHURST   137 M
FROM SYDNEY TO WINDSOR 35
       To PARRAMATTA 14 M
       To LIVERPOOL
       To MACQUARIE TOWNS
To THE SOUTH HEAD
TO THE NORTH HEAD
OF BOTANY BAY